Hooked: How to Build Habit-Forming Products

Atina Amrahs

Published by mds0, 2023.

HOOKED: HOW TO BUILD HABIT-FORMING PRODUCTS

First edition. July 30, 2023.

Copyright © 2023 Atina Amrahs.

ISBN: 979-8223542445

Written by Atina Amrahs.

Table of Contents

Preface 1

1. The Power of Habit 3

2. Crafting Habit-Forming Experiences 6

3. Sparking User Engagement 9

4. Making Users Take the Next Step 12

5. The Art of Creating Addictive Experiences 15

6. Building User Loyalty and Long-term Habits.............. 19

7. Addressing Ethical Concerns of Habit Formation 23

8. Applying the Model to Your Product........................... 26

9. Navigating Digital Addictions 29

10. Creating Compelling User Interfaces 33

11. Nudges and Behavioral Design 36

12. Building Positive Habits and Social Impact 40

13. Overcoming Addictions and Unhealthy Habits 44

14. The Neuroscience of Habit Formation........................ 48

15. From Novice to Habitual 51

16. Gamification and Habit Loops 54

17. Analyzing and Enhancing User Engagement.............. 58

18. Habit-Forming Marketing.. 61

19. Integrating Products into Daily Life 65

20. The Role of Emotions in Habit Building.................... 69

21. Cultivating User Behavior Change.............................. 72

22. The Power of Habitual Engagement 75

23. The Future of Habit-Forming Products 78

24. Building Lasting Habits 81

25. Community and Habit Formation................................ 84

26. Applying Brain Science to Product Development 87

27. Responsibility in Product Design................................ 90

28. Unlocking User Motivation and Commitment 93

29. Data-Driven Habit Building.. 96

30. The Habit-Forming Journey 99

Epilogue 102

Preface

Welcome to "Hooked: How to Build Habit-Forming Products." In this book, we embark on a journey into the captivating world of habit formation and its profound impact on product design, user behavior, and the digital landscape. As product designers, entrepreneurs, and innovators, our goal is to create products that not only capture users' attention but also become an indispensable part of their daily lives. We believe that understanding the principles of habit formation is the key to building products that resonate deeply with users and drive long-term engagement.

In today's fast-paced and hyper-connected world, our digital interactions have become integral to how we live, work, and connect with others. From social media platforms to fitness apps, from productivity tools to language-learning apps, habit-forming products are all around us, subtly shaping our behaviors and routines. The allure of these products lies in their ability to create habits—repeated automatic actions that occur almost instinctively. They become a part of who we are, influencing how we spend our time, make decisions, and pursue our goals.

As we explore the world of habit-forming products, we will delve into the psychology, neuroscience, and design principles that underpin their success. We will uncover the secrets of what makes products sticky, addictive, and integral to users' daily lives. But we must tread carefully, for the power to shape habits comes with great responsibility. Our goal is not to create mindless addiction or manipulate users but to build products that enrich their lives, support their goals, and enhance their well-being.

Our journey through the world of habit-forming products is both enlightening and thought-provoking. We invite you to explore the principles, strategies, and ethical considerations that shape the design and impact of habit-forming products. As we navigate this dynamic landscape, we must remain mindful of the responsibility we bear as product designers—to create products that inspire positive change, enrich users' lives, and cultivate meaningful, lasting habits.

With each chapter, we aim to provide you with valuable insights, actionable strategies, and inspiring success stories to guide you on your quest to build habit-forming products that stand the test of time. By understanding the psychology of habit formation and adopting a user-centric approach, we can create experiences that go beyond mere engagement, becoming an integral and indispensable part of users' lives.

We hope you find "Hooked: How to Build Habit-Forming Products" to be a valuable resource in your pursuit of designing products that resonate deeply with users, foster positive behaviors, and make a lasting impact in the world. May this journey inspire you to embrace the power of habit formation and leverage it to create products that bring joy, empowerment, and meaningful change to the lives of millions.

—**Author**

1. The Power of Habit

To build truly addictive products, we must understand the intricate workings of the human brain and the role habits play in our lives. In this chapter, we explore the power of habit and the psychological hooks that make products irresistible.

The Habit Loop

At the core of habit formation lies the habit loop, a simple yet powerful concept first introduced by Charles Duhigg in "The Power of Habit." The habit loop consists of three key components: the cue, the routine, and the reward. Understanding each element is essential for product designers to create engaging experiences.

1. The Cue: The cue acts as a trigger, signaling the brain to go into automatic mode and initiating the habit loop. Cues can take various forms, such as a notification, an email, a visual stimulus, an emotion, or even a specific time of day. Successful products identify and leverage triggers that align with users' existing routines or emotional states.

For example, the notification sound of a messaging app serves as a cue for users to check their messages. Similarly, when users feel bored or anxious, they may instinctively reach for their social media feed to feel connected or distracted.

2. The Routine: The routine is the actual behavior or action that follows the cue. Once the trigger occurs, users engage in a specific behavior, often without conscious thought. The more a routine is repeated, the more it becomes ingrained in the user's mind, making it more automatic and habitual over time. Product designers aim to make these routines as simple and intuitive as possible. By reducing friction and making the desired behavior easy to perform, users are more likely to follow through.

3. The Reward: The reward is the positive outcome or emotional satisfaction that users experience after completing the routine. It is the key element that reinforces the habit loop. The brain associates the reward with the cue and routine, creating a sense of anticipation and pleasure for the next iteration.

Rewards can take many forms, including social approval, a sense of accomplishment, entertainment, or even a simple dopamine release. Habit-forming products excel at delivering variable rewards, making the user experience unpredictable and compelling. Users become driven to seek out these rewards repeatedly, fueling the habit loop.

The Habit Loop in Product Design

Understanding the habit loop is crucial for designing products that form strong user habits. Product designers can leverage this knowledge to create experiences that resonate deeply with users and keep them engaged.

1. Identifying Triggers: To design effective cues, product designers must gain a deep understanding of their target audience. This involves studying user behavior, conducting interviews, and employing user surveys. By identifying the triggers that align with users' existing habits and emotional states, designers can increase the likelihood of users engaging with the product.

For example, fitness apps might use the time of day as a cue for users to log their workouts. Meditation apps could use users' self-reported stress levels as a cue to encourage mindfulness exercises.

2. Simplifying Routines: The easier it is for users to perform the desired behavior, the more likely they are to engage with the product habitually. Product designers must remove any unnecessary steps and reduce friction in the user journey.

For instance, a meal planning app could streamline the process of adding recipes and ingredients to a shopping list. Social media platforms might allow users to post content with just a few taps, encouraging frequent updates.

3. Delivering Compelling Rewards: To create habit-forming products, designers must provide rewards that deeply resonate with users. These rewards should satisfy users' emotional needs and leave them wanting more.

Variable rewards are particularly effective. For example, a news app could provide users with personalized news articles, tailored to their interests. The anticipation of discovering relevant and interesting content keeps users coming back for more.

Ethical Considerations

While understanding the psychological hooks of habit formation is essential for product designers, it also raises important ethical considerations. The power to shape user behavior comes with significant responsibilities. Designers must be conscious of the impact their products can have on users' lives and avoid exploiting vulnerabilities for short-term gains.

Conclusion

In this chapter, we have explored the power of habit and the psychological hooks that underlie habit-forming products. By understanding the habit loop and its components—the cue, routine, and reward—product designers can create experiences that captivate users and keep them coming back for more. However, it is essential to approach this knowledge with ethical considerations, ensuring that habit-forming products are used to empower and enhance users' lives responsibly. Harnessing the power of habit is a potent tool in the designer's toolkit, one that can lead to the creation of products that have a positive and lasting impact on users' behavior and well-being.

2. Crafting Habit-Forming Experiences

Now, we turn our attention to the core framework that enables designers to create these addictive experiences—the Hook Model. In this chapter, we delve into the four phases of the Hook Model and understand how each stage contributes to the formation of irresistible habits.

Trigger - The First Hook

The Hook Model begins with the trigger, which serves as the first hook to draw users into the product experience. Triggers prompt users to take action, initiating the habit loop we explored in the previous chapter. Triggers can be classified into two types: external triggers and internal triggers.

A. External Triggers: External triggers are cues from the user's environment that prompt them to engage with the product. These cues can be in the form of notifications, emails, app icons, advertisements, or even word-of-mouth recommendations. The key to effective external triggers lies in their ability to be timely, relevant, and attention-grabbing.

For example, a fitness app might send a notification to remind users about their daily workout or a social media platform could use a red notification badge to indicate new messages or updates.

B. Internal Triggers: Internal triggers, on the other hand, originate from within the user. They are associated with emotional states, thoughts, or feelings that lead users to seek out the product experience. Internal triggers often tap into fundamental human needs, such as the need for social connection, information, or entertainment.

Social media platforms are masters at leveraging internal triggers. When users feel bored or lonely, they instinctively open the app to connect with others and fill the emotional void.

Action - The Second Hook

After the trigger has caught the user's attention, the next step is to guide them towards taking action. The action phase of the Hook Model focuses on making the desired behavior as effortless and frictionless as possible. Reducing the gap between the trigger and the action is crucial to driving user engagement.

A. Simplicity: Designers must simplify the action so that users can easily perform the desired behavior without encountering barriers. This may involve reducing the number of steps required, streamlining the user interface, or employing intuitive design elements.

For instance, ride-hailing apps like Uber and Lyft have mastered simplicity by allowing users to request a ride with just a few taps on their smartphones.

B. Clear Call-to-Action: A clear and compelling call-to-action guides users on what to do next. The call to action should be prominently displayed and convey a sense of urgency or value.

For example, e-commerce platforms often use phrases like "Buy Now" or "Limited Time Offer" to encourage immediate action from uscrs.

Variable Reward - The Third Hook

The third phase of the Hook Model is the variable reward, which is a critical driver of habit formation. Unlike fixed rewards that offer the same outcome every time, variable rewards create intrigue and anticipation, keeping users engaged and coming back for more.

A. The Element of Surprise: Variable rewards introduce an element of surprise, making each interaction with the product unique. Users never know exactly what they will get, but they know it could be something valuable or enjoyable.

Social media platforms leverage this principle by presenting users with a mix of content, including updates from friends, entertaining videos, and thought-provoking articles.

B. Dopamine Release: Variable rewards activate the brain's reward system, leading to the release of dopamine, a neurotransmitter associated with pleasure and motivation. This neurological response creates a positive feedback loop, reinforcing the habit loop and driving continued engagement.

Mobile games often use variable rewards to keep players engaged. The uncertainty of getting rare items or rewards after completing tasks keeps players motivated to continue playing.

Investment - The Fourth Hook

The final phase of the Hook Model is the investment phase. In this stage, users put effort, time, or personal data into the product, leading to an increased sense of ownership and attachment.

A. Effort: When users invest effort into a product, they become more committed to it. This commitment fosters a desire to return to the product to maintain the fruits of their labor.

For example, users of note-taking apps may invest time in organizing their notes and creating custom tags. As a result, they become more likely to return to the app for future note-taking needs.

B. Data: Investing personal data, such as preferences, history, or user-generated content, personalizes the experience and strengthens the user's bond with the product. As users invest more data, the product becomes better tailored to their needs and preferences.

Social networking sites encourage users to invest time in creating profiles, sharing photos, and connecting with others. As users add more data, the platform becomes more valuable to them, reinforcing the habit loop.

Conclusion

The Hook Model is a powerful framework for designing habit-forming products. By understanding and implementing triggers, actions, variable rewards, and investments, product designers can create experiences that captivate users and drive continued engagement. However, it is crucial to use this knowledge ethically, ensuring that habit-forming products are designed to add value to users' lives responsibly. When harnessed effectively, the Hook Model can lead to the creation of products that form positive habits, benefiting both users and businesses alike.

3. Sparking User Engagement

Now, we dive deeper into the first phase of the Hook Model—the trigger. Triggers play a crucial role in sparking user engagement and initiating the habit-forming loop. In this chapter, we examine the different types of triggers, their psychological impact on users, and strategies for effectively utilizing triggers to build habit-forming products.

Understanding Triggers

Triggers are stimuli that prompt users to take action. They can be external or internal, and both types have their unique effects on user behavior.

1. External Triggers: External triggers are cues in the user's environment that prompt them to engage with a product or service. These triggers are essential for capturing the user's attention and initiating their interaction with the product. Common examples of external triggers include notifications, email alerts, app icons, advertisements, and word-of-mouth recommendations.

External triggers are particularly effective in getting users to act immediately, as they interrupt their current state and present an opportunity for engagement. When designing habit-forming products, it's crucial to craft external triggers that are timely, relevant, and attention-grabbing.

2. Internal Triggers: Internal triggers, on the other hand, originate from within the user. They are associated with the user's emotions, thoughts, and feelings, and can be powerful motivators for engagement. Unlike external triggers, which rely on the environment, internal triggers are rooted in the user's psychological state and can be more subtle but equally influential.

Internal triggers often tap into fundamental human needs and desires, such as the need for social connection, entertainment, information, or relief from boredom or anxiety. Understanding the user's emotional landscape and identifying these internal triggers is crucial for creating a personalized and engaging user experience.

The Psychological Impact of Triggers

Triggers influence user behavior by tapping into the brain's reward system and creating a sense of anticipation and pleasure. When a trigger is successfully associated with a positive or rewarding experience, it creates a psychological hook that encourages users to seek out the behavior repeatedly.

1. The Brain's Reward System: When users encounter triggers that lead to a positive outcome or reward, such as an interesting article, an entertaining video, or a social interaction, the brain's reward system is activated. This system involves the release of dopamine, a neurotransmitter associated with pleasure and motivation.

The activation of the brain's reward system creates a pleasurable feeling, making users more likely to seek out the behavior again in pursuit of that rewarding experience. Habit-forming products leverage this neurological response by providing users with variable rewards, as discussed in the previous chapters, to keep them engaged and coming back for more.

2. Anticipation and Pleasure: Effective triggers create a sense of anticipation and pleasure in users. The anticipation of a rewarding experience becomes a motivator for action, driving users to engage with the product. Similarly, the pleasure experienced after engaging with the product reinforces the habit loop, making it more likely for users to repeat the behavior in the future.

By understanding the psychological impact of triggers, product designers can craft experiences that leverage these principles to create habits and keep users hooked on their products.

Effective Triggering Strategies

Creating habit-forming products requires careful consideration of the triggering phase. Here are some effective strategies to implement triggers successfully:

1. Contextual Relevance: Triggers must be contextually relevant to the user's needs and preferences. Understanding the user's goals, emotions, and situational context allows designers to craft triggers that resonate with users and prompt them to take action.

For example, a news app might send personalized notifications based on the user's interests and reading habits, ensuring that the trigger is relevant and compelling.

2. Personalization: Personalization is a powerful way to enhance the effectiveness of triggers. By tailoring triggers to each user's behavior and preferences, the product becomes more engaging and relevant to the individual user.

E-commerce platforms often use personalized recommendations based on past purchases or browsing history to trigger user engagement and increase the likelihood of conversion.

3. Timing and Frequency: The timing and frequency of triggers can significantly impact user engagement. Triggers should be timed appropriately to coincide with the user's natural behavior or routine.

For instance, a reminder app that prompts users to take their medication should be set to trigger at the appropriate times of the day when the user is likely to take the medication.

However, designers must be cautious not to overwhelm users with excessive or untimely triggers, as this can lead to irritation or disengagement.

4. Gradual Onboarding: For new users, triggering should be approached with a gradual onboarding process. Overwhelming users with too many triggers at once can lead to a negative user experience and deter them from forming a habit.

Instead, introduce triggers gradually, giving users time to familiarize themselves with the product and its benefits.

5. A/B Testing: A/B testing is a valuable tool to optimize triggers and determine which types of triggers are most effective in driving user engagement. By testing different trigger variations, product designers can gather data and insights on user responses, allowing them to refine and improve triggering strategies.

Conclusion

The triggering phase of the Hook Model is the first step in building habit-forming products. Understanding the different types of triggers—external and internal—and their psychological impact on users is crucial for sparking user engagement. By crafting triggers that are contextually relevant, personalized, and timed appropriately, product designers can create experiences that resonate with users, motivate action, and drive habit formation. Implementing effective triggering strategies lays the foundation for the subsequent phases of the Hook Model, leading to the creation of products that keep users hooked and returning for more.

4. Making Users Take the Next Step

In the Hook Model, the second phase after the trigger is the action—the behavior users take in response to the trigger. This chapter focuses on the crucial role of actionable feedback in driving user engagement during the action phase. Actionable feedback provides users with clear and immediate responses to their actions, creating a sense of progress, accomplishment, and motivation to take the next step. By understanding the principles of actionable feedback, product designers can design more effective and habit-forming products that keep users coming back for more.

The Role of Actionable Feedback

Actionable feedback is the key to turning triggers into meaningful interactions. It is the essential link that connects the user's action to a tangible outcome, reinforcing the habit loop. Without actionable feedback, users may not see the value or impact of their actions, leading to disengagement and abandonment of the product.

Actionable feedback serves several important functions in habit-forming products:

1. Reinforcement: Positive feedback reinforces desired behaviors and encourages users to repeat them. When users receive a reward or positive outcome in response to their actions, it strengthens the connection between the trigger and the behavior, making it more likely for users to engage again in the future.

2. Immediate Gratification: Actionable feedback provides immediate gratification to users, satisfying their desire for instant results or rewards. The faster users see the impact of their actions, the more motivated they are to continue engaging with the product.

3. Progress Tracking: Feedback that shows users their progress towards a goal or achievement provides a sense of accomplishment and progress. This sense of progress encourages users to keep moving forward and take the next step in their journey with the product.

4. User Guidance: Clear feedback guides users on how to use the product effectively. It informs users whether their actions are on the right track or need adjustments, improving the overall user experience and reducing frustration.

Designing Effective Actionable Feedback

To create habit-forming products, designers must carefully consider how to design actionable feedback that encourages user engagement and habit formation. Here are some principles and strategies for designing effective actionable feedback:

1. Real-Time Responses: Actionable feedback should be provided in real-time, as close to the user's action as possible. Immediate responses make users feel that their actions have an impact, increasing their motivation to continue engaging with the product.

For example, in a gaming app, when a user completes a level or achieves a high score, the app should display the results and rewards without delay, providing instant gratification.

2. Visual and Audio Cues: Using visual and audio cues enhances the impact of actionable feedback. Visual cues, such as animations, progress bars, or badges, make the feedback more engaging and understandable.

For instance, a progress bar in a language-learning app can visually show users their language proficiency level, encouraging them to continue learning to reach the next milestone.

3. Meaningful Rewards: The feedback should include meaningful rewards that align with the user's goals and motivations. Rewards can take various forms, such as virtual badges, points, discounts, or access to exclusive content.

For a loyalty program, customers could earn points for each purchase, which they can redeem for discounts or special offers, creating a sense of value and incentive to continue shopping.

4. Clear User Guidance: Actionable feedback should provide clear guidance on what users should do next. This helps users understand their progress and the steps they need to take to achieve their desired outcomes.

For example, in a goal-setting app, actionable feedback could display personalized tips or suggestions on how to make progress towards the user's goals.

5. Error Prevention and Recovery: Feedback should also address errors and mistakes, helping users recover from missteps. Clear feedback on errors and how to correct them reduces frustration and encourages users to try again.

In a form-filling app, if a user enters incorrect information, the app could display an error message with suggestions on how to correct the input.

6. Gradual Complexity: To prevent overwhelming users, gradually introduce more complex feedback as users become more familiar with the product. Gradual complexity ensures that users can grasp the feedback's meaning and relevance at each stage of their journey with the product.

For example, in a fitness tracking app, basic feedback on steps taken could be provided initially, followed by more detailed feedback on distance, calories burned, and heart rate as users become more engaged with the app.

Conclusion

Actionable feedback is a critical component of the Hook Model that drives user engagement during the action phase. By providing clear and immediate responses to user actions, actionable feedback reinforces desired behaviors, offers immediate gratification, tracks progress, and guides users on their journey with the product. When designed effectively, actionable feedback creates a sense of accomplishment and motivation, encouraging users to continue engaging with habit-forming products. By incorporating the principles and strategies of actionable feedback, product designers can create experiences that keep users hooked and coming back for more, ultimately leading to long-term user retention and product success.

5. The Art of Creating Addictive Experiences

In the Hook Model, the third phase after the trigger and action is the variable reward—a key element in creating addictive and habit-forming experiences. Variable rewards are the secret sauce that keeps users coming back for more. They leverage the brain's pleasure-seeking mechanism and create a sense of anticipation, making users crave the next interaction with the product. In this chapter, we explore the art of creating variable rewards and how they drive user engagement in habit-forming products.

Understanding Variable Rewards

Variable rewards are rewards that are not delivered consistently, but rather unpredictably. Unlike fixed rewards, which provide the same outcome every time, variable rewards create intrigue and excitement, keeping users engaged and motivated to continue interacting with the product.

The concept of variable rewards is deeply rooted in psychology, particularly in the field of operant conditioning, which explores how behaviors are reinforced through rewards. Psychologist B.F. Skinner demonstrated that variable reinforcement schedules, where rewards are delivered randomly, lead to higher rates of behavior repetition compared to fixed reinforcement schedules.

This psychological phenomenon is known as the "variable reward effect," and it is the key to understanding why users become hooked on habit-forming products.

The Psychology Behind Variable Rewards

Variable rewards tap into two essential psychological principles:

1. Anticipation: Variable rewards create a sense of anticipation in users. When users receive a reward, their brain releases dopamine, a neurotransmitter associated with pleasure and motivation. However, the anticipation of a reward triggers an even greater dopamine release. The uncertainty and surprise of not knowing when the next reward will come make the experience more exciting and addictive.

In habit-forming products, users come to associate the trigger and action with the possibility of a reward, fueling their motivation to keep engaging with the product.

2. The Zeigarnik Effect: The Zeigarnik Effect is a psychological phenomenon that states that people remember uncompleted or interrupted tasks better than completed ones. In the context of variable rewards, this means that when users experience an unfinished or unrewarded action, they feel a sense of cognitive tension—a desire to complete the task and receive the reward.

This cognitive tension keeps users engaged and coming back to the product to seek closure and resolution, leading to continued interaction and habit formation.

Types of Variable Rewards

Variable rewards can take various forms, and the type of reward offered can significantly impact user engagement. Here are some common types of variable rewards:

1. Content: Content-based variable rewards involve providing users with a diverse range of content that changes over time. This can include new articles, videos, images, or interactive experiences.

Social media platforms excel at using content-based variable rewards by presenting users with an ever-changing feed of updates and posts from friends and influencers.

2. Social Interaction: Social interaction-based variable rewards offer users the opportunity to connect with others, receive feedback, or participate in social validation.

For example, in a dating app, users may receive unpredictable messages or matches, keeping them engaged in the hope of forming new connections.

3. Progress and Achievements: Variable rewards related to progress and achievements involve recognizing and celebrating users' accomplishments. Users receive a sense of accomplishment when they reach a milestone or achieve a goal.

Fitness tracking apps use this strategy by rewarding users with badges or virtual trophies for completing certain fitness challenges or achieving specific targets.

4. Gamification: Gamification-based variable rewards incorporate game-like elements, such as points, levels, and virtual rewards, to make the experience more engaging and enjoyable.

Mobile games often use this strategy, providing users with surprise bonuses, power-ups, or virtual currency at different stages of the game.

5. Discounts and Offers: Variable rewards related to discounts and offers offer users surprise discounts or exclusive offers, encouraging them to keep engaging with the product to uncover these rewards.

E-commerce platforms often use this strategy by sending personalized discounts or flash sales to users based on their browsing or purchase history.

Strategies for Creating Effective Variable Rewards

Designing effective variable rewards requires a deep understanding of the target audience and their motivations. Here are some strategies for creating compelling variable rewards:

1. Personalization: Tailor variable rewards to each user's preferences and behavior. The more personalized the rewards, the more relevant and enticing they will be to the user.

By analyzing user data and behavior, habit-forming products can deliver rewards that align with individual preferences, increasing the likelihood of engagement.

2. Surprise and Unpredictability: The element of surprise is a crucial factor in creating effective variable rewards. Users should not be able to predict when or what rewards they will receive.

Randomizing the timing and type of rewards keeps users curious and excited about the possibilities, encouraging them to keep engaging with the product.

3. Gradual Intensification: To sustain engagement over the long term, gradually intensify the rewards as users become more invested in the product.

Start with smaller, easier-to-achieve rewards in the early stages to build user interest and motivation. As users progress, introduce more significant rewards to keep them hooked.

4. Avoid Overstimulation: While variable rewards are powerful motivators, excessive use can lead to overstimulation and desensitization. Designers must strike a balance between providing rewards and avoiding overwhelming users.

Overstimulation can reduce the impact of rewards and diminish their effectiveness in driving engagement.

5. Encourage User Investment: Encourage users to invest time, effort, or data into the product to enhance their sense of ownership and attachment. The more invested users are, the more motivated they will be to continue engaging with the product to protect and grow their investment.

Social media platforms do this by encouraging users to create and curate their content, making them feel more connected and invested in the platform.

Conclusion

Variable rewards are a powerful tool for creating addictive and habit-forming experiences. By leveraging the psychology of anticipation and the Zeigarnik Effect, variable rewards create a sense of excitement and motivation for users to engage with the product repeatedly.

Designing effective variable rewards involves personalization, surprise, gradual intensification, and careful consideration of user investment. When implemented thoughtfully, variable rewards drive user engagement, strengthen the habit loop, and lead to the creation of habit-forming products that keep users hooked for the long term. By mastering the art of creating variable rewards, product designers can craft experiences that captivate and delight users, ultimately leading to the success and sustainability of their products.

6. Building User Loyalty and Long-term Habits

In the Hook Model, the fourth and final phase after the trigger, action, and variable rewards is the investment. Investment is the process of users putting effort, time, or data into a product, building a sense of ownership and attachment. This chapter explores the role of investment in building user loyalty and fostering long-term habits with habit-forming products. By understanding the principles of investment, product designers can create experiences that keep users engaged and coming back for more, leading to sustained user retention and product success.

The Importance of Investment

Investment is a critical aspect of building habit-forming products. It represents the commitment and effort users put into the product, leading to increased engagement and attachment. When users invest time, energy, or personal data, they become more likely to continue using the product to protect and maximize their investment.

Investment also plays a vital role in forming user habits. As users repeat the habit loop, they become more invested in the product, creating a reinforcing cycle that deepens their commitment and loyalty over time.

Key Elements of Investment

Several key elements contribute to user investment in habit-forming products:

1. Effort: Users invest effort when they spend time learning how to use the product effectively or when they customize their experience to suit their preferences. The effort users put into the product creates a sense of ownership and responsibility, leading to increased loyalty.

2. Data: When users provide personal data, such as preferences, interests, or usage patterns, they enable the product to deliver more personalized and relevant experiences. The more data users invest, the better the product can cater to their individual needs, strengthening the user-product relationship.

3. Content Creation: When users create and contribute content to the product, they become emotionally invested in the platform. Content creation fosters a sense of community and belonging, encouraging users to keep engaging and interacting with others.

4. Social Connections: Investing time in building social connections within the product, such as forming friendships or professional networks, strengthens user loyalty. Social connections make users feel part of a community and motivate them to continue using the product to stay connected.

5. Integration with Daily Routine: When a product becomes integrated into a user's daily routine, it becomes habitual, and the user invests in the product by making it an essential part of their life. This integration creates a strong sense of dependency and loyalty.

Strategies for Encouraging User Investment

Product designers can implement various strategies to encourage user investment and build long-term habits with their products:

1. Onboarding and Personalization: A seamless onboarding process that guides users through the initial setup of the product can encourage early investment. Personalization, such as recommending relevant features or content based on user data, also enhances investment by making the product feel tailor-made for each user.

2. Gamification: Gamification techniques, such as rewarding users for completing tasks or achieving milestones, can drive investment. These rewards create a sense of progress and accomplishment, motivating users to continue engaging with the product.

3. User-Generated Content: Encouraging users to create and share content fosters investment and emotional attachment to the product. User-generated content creates a vibrant community, encouraging users to return to the product to interact with others and showcase their contributions.

4. Social Connectivity: Facilitating social interactions within the product strengthens user investment. Features like messaging, commenting, or collaboration tools create a sense of social belonging and encourage users to keep engaging with others.

5. Integrating with Daily Life: Designers should aim to make the product seamlessly fit into users' daily routines. By becoming an indispensable part of their lives, the product becomes a habit, and users become more invested in using it regularly.

6. Progressive Disclosure: Gradually reveal advanced features or functionalities over time to prevent overwhelming users. Progressive disclosure allows users to

invest effort in learning and mastering the product at their own pace, fostering a sense of ownership and control.

The Impact of Investment on User Habits

User investment is crucial for forming long-term habits with habit-forming products. As users continue to invest effort, time, and data into the product, they build a sense of ownership and attachment. This emotional connection reinforces the habit loop and motivates users to repeat the behavior, leading to sustained engagement and habit formation.

Investment also plays a significant role in user retention. Users who are highly invested in a product are more likely to stay loyal and resist switching to alternatives. The sense of commitment and attachment they have developed makes it difficult for them to abandon the product in favor of a competitor.

Balancing Investment and Friction

While investment is essential for building user loyalty and long-term habits, designers must be mindful of balancing investment with friction. Friction refers to any barriers or obstacles that users encounter while using the product. Excessive friction can deter users from investing in the product, leading to lower engagement and retention.

Product designers must carefully consider where to introduce investment opportunities and where to reduce friction to create a seamless and enjoyable user experience. Minimizing friction in the early stages of user onboarding can encourage users to invest effort and time, laying the foundation for long-term habit formation.

Conclusion

Investment is the final phase of the Hook Model and a key factor in building user loyalty and long-term habits with habit-forming products. When users invest effort, time, data, or social connections in a product, they become emotionally attached and motivated to continue engaging with it.

By implementing strategies such as personalized onboarding, gamification, user-generated content, social connectivity, and integration with daily routines, product designers can encourage user investment and strengthen the habit loop.

Balancing investment with friction is crucial for creating a seamless and enjoyable user experience that fosters sustained engagement and loyalty. Understanding the principles of investment and its impact on user habits empowers product designers to build habit-forming products that keep users hooked and coming back for more.

7. Addressing Ethical Concerns of Habit Formation

In the pursuit of building habit-forming products, it is essential to acknowledge and address the ethical concerns that arise when leveraging psychological principles to create addictive experiences. While habit formation can lead to positive outcomes for both users and businesses, there is a dark side to it—the potential for manipulation, exploitation, and harmful addiction. In this chapter, we delve into the ethical considerations of habit formation, explore the consequences of addictive products, and discuss the responsibility of product designers in creating ethical and responsible user experiences.

The Ethical Dilemma

Habit formation is a powerful tool that can enhance user engagement, satisfaction, and product success. However, the very same techniques that create habit-forming products can also be misused to exploit vulnerabilities and manipulate user behavior. This ethical dilemma lies at the heart of building habit-forming products responsibly.

The responsibility of product designers is to find a balance between creating engaging experiences and ensuring that user well-being and autonomy are upheld. By acknowledging the potential for harm and proactively addressing ethical concerns, product designers can create experiences that add genuine value to users' lives.

Understanding the Consequences of Addictive Products

Addictive products can have significant consequences for users' mental health, well-being, and overall quality of life. Understanding these consequences is crucial for product designers to develop empathy and a sense of responsibility towards their users.

1. Mental Health Impact: Addictive products can contribute to excessive screen time and lead to negative effects on users' mental health. Constant engagement with habit-forming products can result in feelings of anxiety, stress, and social isolation.

2. Attention and Focus: Habit-forming products that demand constant attention and engagement can distract users from important tasks and disrupt their ability to focus on real-life activities.

3. User Manipulation: Dark patterns and manipulative design techniques can deceive and pressure users into taking actions they may not otherwise choose to do. These practices erode user trust and harm the user-product relationship.

4. Privacy Concerns: Products that collect vast amounts of user data for habit formation raise privacy concerns. Users may feel uncomfortable or violated when their personal information is used without their consent.

Addressing Ethical Concerns

To build habit-forming products ethically, product designers must adopt a user-centric approach and prioritize user well-being. Here are some strategies for addressing ethical concerns in habit formation:

1. Transparency: Be transparent about the purpose and intent of the product. Clearly communicate to users how their data will be used and seek their informed consent. Avoid dark patterns and deceptive design practices.

2. User Empowerment: Empower users to have control over their experience with the product. Provide clear settings and preferences that allow users to customize their interactions and opt out of certain features if they wish.

3. Balancing Rewards and Risks: Consider the potential risks and benefits of habit formation for users. Strive to create experiences that offer meaningful rewards while minimizing potential harm and addictive behaviors.

4. Ethical Design Standards: Establish ethical design standards and guidelines within the organization. Encourage open discussions about the ethical implications of product design decisions and involve cross-functional teams in the decision-making process.

5. Regular Auditing: Conduct regular audits of the product's design and impact on users' well-being. Solicit user feedback and conduct usability studies to ensure that the product aligns with ethical principles and user needs.

6. Responsible Use of Data: Collect and use user data responsibly, adhering to relevant privacy regulations. Minimize data collection to only what is necessary for providing a valuable user experience, and prioritize data security and privacy protection.

7. Social Responsibility: Recognize the potential influence and impact of habit-forming products on society. Be mindful of the potential consequences of widespread use and take social responsibility seriously in product design and marketing.

Conclusion

Habit formation is a powerful tool that can drive user engagement and product success. However, it comes with ethical responsibilities. Addressing the dark side of habit formation involves acknowledging the potential consequences of addictive products on user well-being, privacy, and autonomy.

Product designers play a crucial role in shaping user experiences. By adopting a user-centric approach, prioritizing transparency, empowering users, and establishing ethical design standards, designers can build habit-forming products that add genuine value to users' lives without compromising their well-being.

Responsible use of habit formation principles ensures that users are not exploited or manipulated, but rather empowered to make informed choices. By being proactive in addressing ethical concerns, product designers can create experiences that not only hook users but also foster trust, loyalty, and positive long-term relationships between users and their products. Ultimately, ethical habit formation leads to sustainable and meaningful product success while promoting user welfare and societal well-being.

8. Applying the Model to Your Product

Throughout this book, we have explored the Hook Model and its four phases—trigger, action, variable rewards, and investment. We have learned how these psychological principles can be leveraged to build habit-forming products that keep users engaged and coming back for more. In this chapter, we delve into the practical application of the Hook Model, providing a step-by-step blueprint for applying the model to your product and creating experiences that hook users and drive long-term success.

Step 1: Identify Your Target User

The first step in applying the Hook Model to your product is to identify your target user. Understanding your target audience's needs, desires, pain points, and behavioral patterns is crucial for crafting effective triggers and personalized experiences.

Conduct user research, surveys, and interviews to gain insights into your target users' motivations and behaviors. Create user personas to represent different segments of your audience, and use these personas to guide your design decisions.

Step 2: Define the Trigger

The trigger is the starting point of the Hook Model. It is the cue that prompts users to take action and engage with your product. To define your trigger, consider the following:

1. External Triggers: Identify external cues in your user's environment that can prompt them to interact with your product. This could be push notifications, email alerts, social media posts, or word-of-mouth recommendations.

2. Internal Triggers: Understand the internal triggers that tap into your user's emotions, desires, and needs. Internal triggers can be related to boredom, social connection, fear of missing out (FOMO), or the desire for convenience.

Step 3: Design the Action

The action is the behavior users take in response to the trigger. To design the action, consider the following:

1. Simplicity: Keep the action simple and easy to perform. Reduce friction and barriers that might prevent users from taking the desired action.

2. Clear Feedback: Provide clear and immediate feedback in response to the user's action. This feedback can be in the form of visual cues, progress indicators, or rewards.

3. Gradual Onboarding: For new users, design a gradual onboarding process that introduces them to the product's features and benefits step by step.

Step 4: Implement Variable Rewards

Variable rewards are essential for creating addictive experiences. To implement variable rewards, consider the following:

1. Diversity of Rewards: Offer a diverse range of rewards, such as content, social interactions, achievements, and discounts. This ensures that different users are motivated by different types of rewards.

2. Randomization: Randomize the delivery of rewards to create a sense of anticipation and excitement. Avoid predictable patterns, as they can lead to habituation and reduced engagement.

3. Personalization: Personalize the rewards based on each user's behavior, preferences, and progress. Tailored rewards increase their relevance and effectiveness.

Step 5: Encourage User Investment

User investment is crucial for building long-term habits and loyalty. To encourage user investment, consider the following:

1. Customization: Allow users to customize their experience, such as setting preferences, personalizing their profiles, or choosing themes.

2. User-Generated Content: Encourage users to create and share content within the product. User-generated content fosters a sense of ownership and community.

3. Social Connectivity: Facilitate social interactions and connections within the product. Social features create a sense of belonging and attachment.

Step 6: Test, Iterate, and Optimize

Building habit-forming products is an iterative process. Continuously test and gather feedback from users to optimize your product's hook. Use A/B testing to experiment with different triggers, rewards, and investment strategies.

Analyze user data to understand user behavior and identify patterns that can inform your design decisions. Iterate your product based on the insights gained from testing and data analysis.

Step 7: Monitor and Address Ethical Concerns

As you apply the Hook Model to your product, be mindful of ethical considerations and potential consequences of habit formation. Regularly monitor your product's impact on user well-being and privacy.

Be prepared to make adjustments to your design or business practices if you identify any harmful effects or unintended consequences. Prioritize user well-being over short-term gains, and demonstrate a commitment to responsible product design.

Conclusion

The Hook Model provides a powerful framework for building habit-forming products that engage users and drive long-term success. By applying the model to your product and following the blueprint outlined in this chapter, you can create experiences that hook users, foster loyalty, and add genuine value to their lives.

Remember to start by identifying your target user and understanding their needs and motivations. Design triggers that resonate with your users, and create actions that are simple and rewarding. Implement variable rewards to create a sense of anticipation and excitement, and encourage user investment to build lasting habits.

As you implement the Hook Model, always keep ethical considerations at the forefront of your design decisions. Prioritize user well-being and strive to create experiences that empower and enrich your users' lives.

Building habit-forming products is a continuous journey of testing, iterating, and optimizing. Be open to feedback, data-driven insights, and new opportunities for improvement. By combining the principles of the Hook Model with a user-centric and ethical approach, you can create products that not only hook users but also contribute positively to their well-being and happiness.

9. Navigating Digital Addictions

As we immerse ourselves in a digitally connected world, the prevalence of technology in our daily lives continues to grow. Smartphones, social media, gaming, and other digital platforms have become integral parts of our routines, offering convenience, entertainment, and social connectivity. However, the constant presence of technology also raises concerns about digital addictions and their impact on our well-being. In this chapter, we explore the phenomenon of being "hooked on technology," the psychological mechanisms that underlie digital addictions, and strategies to navigate this complex landscape responsibly.

The Allure of Digital Products

Digital products are designed to be engaging and habit-forming. They leverage psychological principles, such as the Hook Model, to create addictive experiences that keep users coming back for more. The convenience, novelty, and immediate rewards offered by technology make it easy for users to fall into the habit of using digital products excessively.

The Psychology of Digital Addictions

Digital addictions are driven by several psychological mechanisms, including:

1. Dopamine Release: Engaging with technology and receiving notifications, likes, or rewards trigger the release of dopamine in the brain—a neurotransmitter associated with pleasure and reward. The anticipation of positive outcomes keeps users hooked and motivated to continue engaging with digital products.

2. FOMO (Fear of Missing Out): Social media platforms, in particular, exploit the fear of missing out by providing users with a constant stream of updates and content from their social circle. Users fear missing out on important news, events, or social interactions, which compels them to stay connected to their devices.

3. Endless Scroll: The endless scroll feature in many digital products, such as social media feeds or news websites, creates an infinite loop of content. Users can keep scrolling indefinitely, leading to excessive usage and time spent on these platforms.

4. Personalization and Algorithmic Recommendations: Digital products use algorithms to personalize content and recommendations based on user behavior and preferences. This personalization creates a sense of relevance and relevance, encouraging users to keep engaging with the platform.

5. Variable Rewards: The variable rewards implemented in digital products, as described in the Hook Model, keep users addicted to the unpredictability of rewards and the possibility of discovering something new or exciting.

The Impact of Digital Addictions

Digital addictions can have various negative consequences on individuals and society, including:

1. Mental Health Issues: Excessive use of technology has been linked to mental health issues such as anxiety, depression, and loneliness. Constant comparison with others on social media and the pressure to curate a perfect online image can contribute to feelings of inadequacy and self-doubt.

2. Decreased Productivity: Digital addictions can lead to decreased productivity and attention span. Constant interruptions from notifications and the lure of online distractions can make it difficult to focus on important tasks.

3. Sleep Disturbances: Excessive screen time, especially before bedtime, can disrupt sleep patterns and lead to sleep disturbances. The blue light emitted by screens can interfere with the production of the sleep hormone melatonin.

4. Social Isolation: While digital products promise social connectivity, excessive use can paradoxically lead to social isolation as users become more engrossed in their virtual lives than in real-world interactions.

Strategies to Navigate Digital Addictions

As technology continues to play an increasingly significant role in our lives, it is crucial to adopt strategies to navigate digital addictions responsibly. Here are some approaches to promoting a healthier relationship with technology:

1. Digital Detox: Periodically disconnect from digital devices and platforms to give yourself a break from constant connectivity. Set aside designated times each day or week to be device-free and engage in activities that do not involve screens.

2. Mindful Technology Use: Practice mindfulness when using technology. Be aware of how much time you spend on digital platforms and how they make

you feel. Set intentional goals for technology use and be mindful of your emotional responses to digital content.

3. Set Boundaries: Establish clear boundaries for technology use, especially during meals, family time, or before bedtime. Create technology-free zones in your home or workplace to promote healthy interactions and focused activities.

4. Disable Notifications: Limit the distractions caused by notifications by disabling non-essential alerts. This helps reduce the constant urge to check devices and fosters more focused and productive engagement with technology.

5. Curate Your Digital Environment: Be intentional about the digital content you consume. Unfollow or mute accounts that evoke negative emotions or comparison anxiety. Curate your social media feeds to include content that adds value and positivity to your life.

6. Prioritize Real-World Connections: Balance online interactions with real-world connections. Make time for face-to-face interactions with family and friends to strengthen social bonds and combat feelings of social isolation.

7. Practice Digital Sabbaths: Set aside a day or part of a day each week when you completely disconnect from digital devices. Use this time for introspection, relaxation, and engaging in activities that bring joy and fulfillment.

8. Educate and Empower: Educate yourself and others about the potential risks of excessive technology use and digital addictions. Encourage open conversations about responsible technology use and the importance of setting healthy boundaries.

Conclusion

As technology continues to evolve and play an ever-increasing role in our lives, it is essential to navigate the landscape of digital addictions responsibly. Digital products are designed to be habit-forming, and users may find themselves hooked on technology without even realizing it.

By understanding the psychological mechanisms that underlie digital addictions and adopting strategies to promote mindful and intentional technology use, we can develop a healthier relationship with technology. Digital detox, setting boundaries, and prioritizing real-world connections are some of the approaches that can help us strike a balance between the benefits of technology and our well-being.

As product designers and creators of habit-forming products, we also have a responsibility to design ethically and prioritize user well-being over short-term gains. By creating experiences that add genuine value to users' lives without exploiting their vulnerabilities, we can contribute to a more balanced and positive relationship with technology for everyone.

10. Creating Compelling User Interfaces

In the quest to build habit-forming products, user interface (UI) design plays a crucial role. The user interface is the bridge between the user and the product, shaping the user experience and influencing user behavior. In this chapter, we explore the principles and strategies of habit-forming design, focusing on creating compelling user interfaces that engage users, drive habit formation, and enhance the overall user experience.

Understanding Habit-Forming Design

Habit-forming design is about crafting user interfaces that encourage repeated interactions and foster long-term engagement. It leverages psychological principles and user-centered design to create experiences that keep users coming back for more. The goal is to create a seamless and enjoyable user experience that aligns with users' needs and motivations, leading to the formation of positive habits.

Key Principles of Habit-Forming Design

1. Simplicity: Simplicity is a fundamental principle of habit-forming design. Keep the user interface clean, intuitive, and easy to navigate. Avoid clutter and unnecessary complexity, as they can lead to confusion and frustration.

2. Clear Call-to-Action (CTA): Use clear and compelling calls-to-action that prompt users to take the desired actions. CTAs should be visually prominent, concise, and aligned with the user's goals.

3. Visual Hierarchy: Establish a clear visual hierarchy in the user interface to guide users' attention and focus. Use visual cues such as size, color, and contrast to highlight important elements and actions.

4. Feedback and Animation: Provide immediate and informative feedback to users when they perform actions. Utilize animations and transitions to enhance the user experience and create a sense of responsiveness.

5. Personalization: Tailor the user interface to individual users' preferences and behavior. Personalization makes the product feel more relevant and engaging to each user, increasing the likelihood of habit formation.

6. Progressive Disclosure: Gradually reveal features and information to users as they become more familiar with the product. Progressive disclosure prevents overwhelming users with too much information upfront.

7. Consistency: Maintain consistency in the user interface design throughout the product. Consistency creates a sense of familiarity and helps users build mental models of how the product works.

Strategies for Habit-Forming Design

1. Visual Cues for Triggers: Incorporate visual cues that serve as triggers for users to initiate actions. For example, a prominent "Play" button can trigger users to start watching a video or a notification badge can prompt users to check their messages.

2. Seamless Onboarding: Design a seamless onboarding process that introduces users to the product's features and benefits gradually. A smooth onboarding experience reduces friction and encourages users to explore the product further.

3. Gamification Elements: Incorporate gamification elements, such as progress bars, badges, or rewards, to motivate users and reinforce their engagement. Gamification adds an element of fun and accomplishment to the user experience.

4. Variable Rewards Feedback: Use visual feedback to enhance the impact of variable rewards. When users receive rewards, provide visually appealing animations or sounds that create a positive emotional response.

5. Social Proof and Social Connectivity: Integrate social proof elements, such as user reviews or testimonials, to build trust and encourage users to engage with the product. Incorporate features that promote social connectivity and interaction to foster a sense of community.

6. Micro-Interactions: Implement micro-interactions throughout the user interface to provide subtle feedback and create a delightful user experience. Micro-interactions, such as subtle button animations or hover effects, add personality and engagement to the product.

7. Personalized Recommendations: Leverage user data to offer personalized recommendations and content. Personalization increases relevance and encourages users to continue interacting with the product.

8. Emphasis on Investment: Design the user interface to highlight investment opportunities, such as customization options or user-generated content. Emphasizing investment encourages users to put effort into the product and fosters long-term loyalty.

Testing and Iterating the User Interface

Building a habit-forming user interface is an iterative process that requires continuous testing and refinement. User feedback, usability testing, and data analysis play essential roles in improving the user experience.

1. Usability Testing: Conduct usability testing to observe how users interact with the interface and identify pain points or areas of confusion. Use the insights gained from testing to make necessary adjustments and improvements.

2. A/B Testing: Perform A/B testing to compare different design variations and identify which design elements are most effective in driving user engagement and habit formation.

3. Analytics and Data Analysis: Analyze user data to understand how users interact with the product and identify patterns of user behavior. Data-driven insights can inform design decisions and help optimize the user interface for better engagement.

Conclusion

Habit-forming design is the key to creating compelling user interfaces that drive user engagement, foster habit formation, and contribute to the success of habit-forming products. By understanding the principles of habit-forming design and implementing strategies such as simplicity, clear CTAs, personalization, and progressive disclosure, product designers can create experiences that keep users coming back for more.

A user-centric approach, continuous testing, and data analysis are essential for refining the user interface and optimizing it for better engagement and habit formation. By prioritizing user needs, preferences, and motivations, habit-forming design can lead to a seamless and enjoyable user experience that keeps users hooked and fosters long-term loyalty to the product.

11. Nudges and Behavioral Design

In the world of habit-forming products, understanding human behavior and decision-making is key to creating experiences that hook users and drive engagement. Nudges and behavioral design are powerful techniques that product designers can use to influence user decisions subtly. In this chapter, we explore the principles of nudges, the psychology behind behavioral design, and how these techniques can be leveraged responsibly to build habit-forming products.

Understanding Nudges

Nudges are subtle changes in the design or presentation of choices that influence people's behavior without restricting their freedom of choice. Nudges work by altering the context in which choices are presented, making certain options more appealing or guiding users toward desired behaviors. The concept of nudging was popularized by Nobel laureate Richard H. Thaler and legal scholar Cass R. Sunstein in their book "Nudge: Improving Decisions About Health, Wealth, and Happiness."

Key Principles of Nudges

1. Default Options: Nudges often use default options to influence user behavior. The default option is the choice that users would make if they did not actively select an alternative. By setting a particular option as the default, designers can increase the likelihood that users will choose that option.

2. Social Norms: Nudges leverage social norms to encourage certain behaviors. People tend to follow what others are doing, so presenting information about the behavior of others can influence user decisions.

3. Anchoring: Anchoring involves presenting a reference point or starting value that influences subsequent judgments or decisions. By providing an anchor value, designers can influence users' perception of other options.

4. Salience and Positioning: Nudges use salience and positioning to draw attention to specific options or information. By making certain choices more prominent or visually appealing, designers can influence users' decision-making.

5. Feedback and Comparison: Providing feedback and allowing users to compare options can influence their decisions. Feedback helps users

understand the consequences of their choices, and comparison enables them to make more informed decisions.

Psychology of Behavioral Design

Behavioral design is rooted in principles of psychology that explain how people think, make decisions, and respond to different stimuli. Several psychological theories and biases are commonly employed in behavioral design:

1. Loss Aversion: People tend to be more motivated to avoid losses than to acquire equivalent gains. Behavioral design can use loss aversion to nudge users toward desired behaviors by highlighting potential losses associated with certain choices.

2. Endowment Effect: The endowment effect is the tendency for people to value something more highly merely because they own it. Behavioral design can leverage this effect by making users feel ownership or attachment to certain features or content within the product.

3. Confirmation Bias: Confirmation bias is the tendency to favor information that confirms pre-existing beliefs or attitudes. Behavioral design can nudge users by presenting information that aligns with their existing beliefs or desired outcomes.

4. Scarcity: The scarcity principle suggests that people value things more when they perceive them to be scarce or limited. Behavioral design can create a sense of scarcity by offering time-limited deals or exclusive content.

5. Priming: Priming is the process by which exposure to one stimulus influences a person's response to a subsequent stimulus. Behavioral design can prime users by presenting certain cues or information that influence their subsequent choices.

Ethical Considerations in Behavioral Design

While nudges and behavioral design can be powerful tools for driving user engagement and habit formation, it is crucial to consider the ethical implications of these techniques. The responsible behavioral design prioritizes user well-being and respects users' autonomy.

1. Transparency: Be transparent about the use of nudges and behavioral design techniques. Clearly communicate to users how their choices are influenced and allow them to opt out if they wish.

2. No Coercion: Avoid using nudges to manipulate or coerce users into making decisions that may not align with their best interests. Nudges should not

restrict users' freedom of choice but rather guide them toward beneficial outcomes.

3. User Empowerment: Empower users to have control over their decisions. Allow users to customize their experience and preferences, and provide clear options for opting out of nudges.

4. Beneficial Outcomes: Ensure that nudges are designed to promote positive and beneficial outcomes for users. Focus on nudges that encourage healthy behaviors, promote well-being, and add value to users' lives.

Examples of Nudges in Habit-Forming Products

1. Default Settings: Setting certain options as default can nudge users toward desired behaviors. For example, in a productivity app, setting the option to receive daily reminders as the default may encourage users to stay organized and focused.

2. Social Proof: Displaying the number of users who have taken a certain action can leverage social norms to encourage others to follow suit. For example, showing the number of people who have donated to a cause can nudge others to contribute as well.

3. Anchoring: Presenting a higher-priced option first can anchor users' perception of the value of other options. For example, a software subscription plan might present a premium option first, making other plans seem more affordable in comparison.

4. Scarcity and Limited Time Offers: Creating a sense of scarcity or offering time-limited deals can nudge users to take immediate action. For example, an e-commerce site might display a "Limited Time Offer" banner to encourage users to make a purchase.

5. Feedback and Progress Tracking: Providing feedback on users' progress can nudge them to continue engaging with a product. For example, a fitness app that displays weekly progress and achievements can motivate users to stay committed to their fitness goals.

Conclusion

Nudges and behavioral design are powerful tools for product designers seeking to create habit-forming products. By understanding the principles of nudges and leveraging psychological insights, designers can influence user decisions and drive long-term engagement.

However, with great power comes great responsibility. Ethical considerations must always guide the use of nudges and behavioral design techniques. Responsible behavioral design prioritizes user well-being, respects users' autonomy, and promotes positive outcomes.

By adopting a user-centric and ethical approach to behavioral design, product designers can create experiences that not only hook users but also add genuine value to their lives. Nudges, when used responsibly, can be a force for good, empowering users to make informed decisions and fostering positive habits that lead to a more fulfilling user experience.

12. Building Positive Habits and Social Impact

In the pursuit of building habit-forming products, there is an opportunity to use these techniques for social good. Habit formation can be harnessed to drive positive behaviors, promote well-being, and create social impact. In this chapter, we explore how product designers can apply the principles of habit formation to build products that inspire positive habits and contribute to meaningful societal change.

The Power of Positive Habits

Habits play a significant role in shaping human behavior. Positive habits can lead to personal growth, improved well-being, and increased productivity. By understanding the mechanisms of habit formation, product designers can design experiences that encourage users to adopt and maintain positive habits.

Key Principles of Building Positive Habits

1. Identifying Positive Behaviors: The first step in building positive habits is to identify the desired behaviors that align with the product's purpose and social impact goals. Positive behaviors could include exercise, meditation, learning, volunteering, or sustainable practices.

2. Triggers for Positive Actions: Design triggers that prompt users to engage in positive behaviors. Triggers can be external, such as reminders or notifications, or internal, tapping into users' intrinsic motivations and emotions.

3. Making Actions Easy: Simplify the process of engaging in positive behaviors. Reduce friction and barriers that may hinder users from adopting the desired habits. Provide clear instructions and support to make it easy for users to take action.

4. Rewarding Positive Actions: Implement variable rewards to reinforce positive behaviors. Celebrate users' progress, achievements, and milestones to create a sense of accomplishment and motivation to continue the positive habits.

5. Social Support and Connectivity: Foster a sense of community and social support around positive habits. Incorporate features that enable users to share their progress, encourage, and collaborate with others pursuing similar goals.

6. Tracking and Progress Monitoring: Enable users to track their progress and monitor their positive habits. Progress tracking provides feedback and helps users stay accountable to their goals.

7. Feedback and Positive Reinforcement: Provide positive feedback and reinforcement when users engage in positive behaviors. Positive reinforcement strengthens the association between the behavior and the positive outcomes, making the habit more likely to be repeated.

Case Studies: Positive Habit-Forming Products

1. Fitness and Wellness Apps: Fitness and wellness apps use habit-forming principles to encourage users to adopt healthy habits such as regular exercise, meditation, or healthy eating. They use triggers like notifications and reminders, provide progress tracking and rewards for achievements, and foster social support through community features.

2. Learning Platforms: Learning platforms leverage habit formation to encourage consistent learning behaviors. They utilize triggers like email reminders or personalized recommendations, offer rewards for completing courses or quizzes, and provide progress tracking to monitor learners' achievements.

3. Sustainable Lifestyle Apps: Apps promoting sustainable practices and eco-friendly behaviors use habit-forming techniques to nudge users toward environmentally conscious actions. They employ triggers like eco-tips and reminders, provide rewards for adopting green habits, and foster a sense of community around sustainability.

4. Charity and Donation Platforms: Charity and donation platforms leverage habit formation to encourage regular giving and philanthropic behaviors. They use triggers like fundraising campaigns and donation reminders, provide social proof of others' contributions, and offer feedback on the impact of donations.

Creating Social Impact Through Positive Habits

1. Addressing Social Issues: Product designers have the opportunity to address pressing social issues through habit-forming products. By focusing on positive habits that contribute to societal well-being, such as health, education, environmental sustainability, and social inclusion, these products can have a significant positive impact.

2. Behavioral Change for Public Good: Habit-forming products can be used to drive behavioral change for the public good. For example, public health

initiatives can leverage habit formation to encourage vaccination, handwashing, or healthy eating habits.

3. Supporting Personal Growth: Habit-forming products can support users in their personal growth journeys. By fostering habits that promote self-improvement, resilience, and well-being, these products can empower users to lead more fulfilling lives.

4. Fostering Social Connection: Habit-forming products that encourage positive social habits can foster a sense of connection and community. By bringing people together around shared goals and interests, these products can combat feelings of isolation and promote social cohesion.

Ethical Considerations in Building Positive Habits

While using habit-forming techniques for social impact is commendable, product designers must approach this endeavor ethically and responsibly.

1. User Well-Being: Prioritize user well-being over short-term engagement or business goals. Ensure that positive habit-forming products are designed to add genuine value to users' lives and contribute positively to their well-being.

2. Informed Consent: Be transparent about the intentions and mechanisms of habit formation used in the product. Obtain users' informed consent, allowing them to make an informed choice about participating in the habit-forming experience.

3. Avoiding Manipulation: Avoid using habit-forming techniques to manipulate or exploit users. Encourage positive behaviors through empowerment and motivation rather than coercion.

4. Privacy and Data Security:

Handle user data responsibly and ethically. Protect users' privacy and adhere to relevant data protection regulations.

5. Monitoring Impact: Regularly monitor the impact of positive habit-forming products on users and society. Be prepared to make adjustments or address unintended consequences that may arise.

Conclusion

Habit formation is a powerful tool that can be harnessed for social good. By understanding the principles of habit formation and leveraging behavioral design techniques, product designers can create experiences that inspire positive behaviors, promote well-being, and contribute to meaningful societal change.

The key to building positive habit-forming products lies in identifying positive behaviors, designing triggers and rewards that motivate users, fostering social support, and empowering users to make a positive impact in their lives and communities.

As product designers, we have the opportunity and responsibility to use habit-forming techniques for good, empowering users to adopt positive habits that lead to personal growth, social impact, and a more fulfilling and meaningful existence. By prioritizing user well-being, transparency, and ethical considerations, we can create habit-forming products that not only hook users but also make a positive difference in the world.

13. Overcoming Addictions and Unhealthy Habits

While habit-forming products can bring great value and convenience to our lives, they also have the potential to lead to addictions and unhealthy habits. In this chapter, we explore the challenges of breaking free from addictive behaviors and unhealthy habits that may arise from using habit-forming products. We'll delve into the psychology of addiction, the impact of technology on behavior, and strategies to overcome addictions and regain control of our lives.

Understanding Addiction and Unhealthy Habits

Addiction is a complex psychological and physiological condition characterized by compulsive behavior despite negative consequences. Unhealthy habits, though not always classified as addictions, can still have detrimental effects on our well-being and daily functioning. The addictive nature of certain habit-forming products can lead to overuse and dependency, causing individuals to feel trapped in a cycle of behavior they cannot control.

The Role of Habit-Forming Products in Addiction

Habit-forming products can contribute to addiction and unhealthy habits in several ways:

1. Dopamine-driven Rewards: The variable rewards and feedback mechanisms in habit-forming products trigger the release of dopamine in the brain. Dopamine is a neurotransmitter associated with pleasure and reward, reinforcing the desire to engage with the product repeatedly.

2. Escapism and Coping Mechanisms: Habit-forming products can become coping mechanisms for stress, anxiety, or boredom. Users may turn to these products to escape from negative emotions, creating a cycle of dependency.

3. Social Pressure: The fear of missing out (FOMO) and the pressure to stay connected with others on social media can drive excessive use of habit-forming products, leading to unhealthy habits.

4. Gaming and Gambling: Some habit-forming products, such as video games and gambling platforms, are designed to be highly addictive. These products exploit psychological principles to keep users engaged for extended periods, leading to potential addiction.

The Impact of Technology on Behavior

The widespread use of technology and habit-forming products has changed the way we interact with the world and with each other. It has also influenced our behavior in various ways:

1. Attention and Focus: Constant notifications and distractions from habit-forming products can lead to decreased attention spans and reduced ability to focus on important tasks.

2. Sleep Disruptions: Excessive screen time, especially before bedtime, can disrupt sleep patterns and lead to sleep disturbances.

3. Social Isolation: While habit-forming products promise social connectivity, excessive use can lead to social isolation as users become more engrossed in their virtual lives than in real-world interactions.

4. Decline in Physical Activity: Habit-forming products that encourage sedentary behaviors, such as extended screen time, can contribute to a decline in physical activity.

Strategies to Overcome Addictions and Unhealthy Habits

1. Awareness and Acceptance: The first step in overcoming addiction and unhealthy habits is to become aware of the problem and accept that it exists. Acknowledge the impact of habit-forming products on your behavior and well-being.

2. Set Boundaries: Establish clear boundaries for technology use, especially for habit-forming products. Set designated times for usage and create technology-free zones to promote a healthy balance.

3. Digital Detox: Consider taking periodic digital detoxes to disconnect from habit-forming products and technology. Use this time for reflection, relaxation, and engaging in offline activities.

4. Seek Support: Reach out for support from friends, family, or professionals if you feel overwhelmed by addiction or unhealthy habits. Talking to others about your struggles can be empowering and may provide valuable insights and guidance.

5. Mindfulness and Self-Reflection: Practice mindfulness to become more aware of your thoughts, feelings, and behaviors when using habit-forming products. Engage in self-reflection to understand the underlying motivations behind your usage patterns.

6. Replace Unhealthy Habits: Identify alternative activities that can replace unhealthy habits. Engaging in hobbies, physical activities, or spending quality

time with loved ones can be positive alternatives to excessive use of habit-forming products.

7. Seek Professional Help: If addiction becomes severe or interferes with daily life, consider seeking professional help from therapists, counselors, or addiction support groups.

Promoting Responsible Design for User Well-Being

Product designers also have a significant role in promoting responsible design to prioritize user well-being and prevent addiction:

1. Ethical Design: Design products that prioritize user well-being over maximizing engagement. Avoid using manipulative techniques that exploit users' vulnerabilities.

2. Transparent Design: Be transparent about the intentions and mechanisms of habit formation used in the product. Inform users about the potentially addictive nature of the product.

3. Empower Users: Empower users to customize their experience and set their preferences, including options to control notifications and limit usage.

4. User Education: Educate users about the impact of technology on behavior and well-being. Provide resources and information on responsible technology use.

5. Responsible Marketing: Avoid aggressive marketing tactics that pressure users into excessive usage. Promote the product's value and benefits honestly.

Conclusion

Habit-forming products can be both beneficial and challenging. While they enhance our lives and offer convenience, they also have the potential to lead to addiction and unhealthy habits. As users, it is essential to be aware of the impact of habit-forming products on our behavior and well-being.

Breaking free from addictive behaviors and unhealthy habits requires self-awareness, self-reflection, and the implementation of strategies to regain control. Setting boundaries, seeking support, and practicing mindfulness can be effective in overcoming addiction and fostering a healthy relationship with technology.

As product designers, it is our responsibility to create experiences that prioritize user well-being and promote positive behaviors. By designing ethically, transparently, and responsibly, we can build habit-forming products that add genuine value to users' lives while safeguarding against the potential risks of addiction and unhealthy habits. Together, we can harness the power of habit formation for good and ensure that technology enriches our lives without compromising our well-being.

14. The Neuroscience of Habit Formation

The formation of habits is a fascinating and intricate process deeply rooted in the brain's neural pathways. As product designers seeking to build habit-forming products, understanding the neuroscience behind habit formation is crucial. In this chapter, we delve into the science of habit formation, explore the brain's role in shaping habits, and discuss the implications of these insights for building successful habit-forming products.

The Habit Loop: Cue, Routine, Reward

At the core of habit formation is the habit loop, a neurological pattern that consists of three key elements: cue, routine, and reward. This loop was first identified by Charles Duhigg, author of "The Power of Habit." Understanding each component is vital to comprehending how habits are formed and how they can be influenced.

1. Cue: The cue is a trigger or a prompt that initiates a habitual behavior. It could be a specific time, location, emotional state, or even an external stimulus. Cues signal the brain to activate the habit and prepare for the routine that follows.

2. Routine: The routine is the actual habitual behavior that follows the cue. This is the behavior that has been repeated consistently over time, often without much conscious thought or decision-making.

3. Reward: The reward is the positive reinforcement or benefit that follows the completion of the routine. It can be tangible, such as a treat, or intangible, such as a feeling of accomplishment or relief. Rewards reinforce the habit loop, making it more likely for the behavior to be repeated in the future.

Neuroplasticity and Habit Formation

The brain's ability to adapt and change in response to experiences is known as neuroplasticity. Habit formation is closely linked to neuroplasticity, as repeated behaviors strengthen neural connections associated with the habit loop. Over time, these connections become more efficient and automatic, leading to the development of habits.

1. Basal Ganglia: The basal ganglia is a brain region involved in habit formation and procedural learning. It plays a critical role in turning actions into automatic habits by storing cue-routine-reward associations.

2. Striatum: The striatum, a part of the basal ganglia, receives signals from the cortex and plays a significant role in habit formation. As habits become more ingrained, the striatum takes over the control of habitual behaviors from the prefrontal cortex.

3. Prefrontal Cortex: The prefrontal cortex is responsible for decision-making, planning, and conscious control. As habits develop, the prefrontal cortex becomes less involved in regulating the behavior, allowing habits to run on autopilot.

Implications for Building Habit-Forming Products

Understanding the neuroscience of habit formation has significant implications for product designers aiming to build habit-forming products. Here are some key insights to consider:

1. Creating Strong Cues: Design products with clear and consistent cues that trigger the desired habits. These cues should be easily recognizable and closely associated with the intended behavior.

2. Reinforcing Rewards: Ensure that the routine is followed by a rewarding experience. This positive reinforcement strengthens the habit loop and makes the behavior more likely to be repeated.

3. Repetition and Consistency: Repeated exposure to the habit loop is essential for forming strong habits. Design products that encourage regular and consistent usage to reinforce the neural connections associated with the habit.

4. Minimizing Decision-Making: Streamline the user experience to minimize decision-making and cognitive effort. A seamless and intuitive interface reduces the reliance on the prefrontal cortex and encourages habitual behaviors.

5. Personalization: Leverage user data to personalize the habit loop for individual users. Tailored experiences are more likely to resonate with users and drive habit formation.

6. Gradual Progression: Allow users to start small and gradually build up to more complex habits. Gradual progression helps users avoid overwhelm and increases the likelihood of successful habit formation.

Ethical Considerations in Habit-Forming Design

While leveraging neuroscience insights to build habit-forming products can be powerful, it also comes with ethical responsibilities:

1. Transparency: Be transparent with users about the design elements that encourage habit formation. Clearly communicate the intended behavior changes and allow users to make informed choices.

2. User Control: Empower users to have control over their habits and the information they share. Provide options to opt out of habit-forming features and personalize their experience.

3. Responsible Use of Data: Handle user data responsibly and ethically. Ensure data privacy and security to protect users' sensitive information.

4. Promote Well-Being: Prioritize user well-being over maximizing engagement or business goals. Design products that encourage positive behaviors and support users' mental and physical health.

Conclusion

The neuroscience of habit formation provides valuable insights into how the brain forms habits and why certain behaviors become automatic and ingrained. As product designers, understanding these neural mechanisms is crucial for building habit-forming products that resonate with users and drive positive behavior change.

By creating strong cues, reinforcing rewards, and encouraging repetition and consistency, product designers can facilitate the development of habits that add value to users' lives. Personalization, gradual progression, and minimizing decision-making can further enhance the habit-forming experience.

However, ethical considerations must always guide the design process. Transparent communication, user control, responsible data use, and promoting user well-being are paramount in building habit-forming products that serve users' best interests.

In summary, leveraging the neuroscience of habit formation responsibly empowers product designers to create experiences that align with users' needs and goals, fostering positive behaviors and enhancing user satisfaction. With this knowledge, designers can build habit-forming products that not only hook users but also contribute to their overall well-being and happiness.

15. From Novice to Habitual

The onboarding process is a critical phase in the user's journey, where they transition from being a novice to becoming a habitual user of a product. Effective onboarding sets the foundation for habit formation, as it guides users through the initial experience and introduces them to the product's value and features. In this chapter, we explore the importance of onboarding in building habit-forming products, key principles for successful onboarding, and strategies to ensure users progress from novice to habitual users.

The Significance of Onboarding in Habit Formation

Onboarding is the user's first interaction with a product, and it significantly impacts their initial impression and likelihood of continued usage. A successful onboarding experience is crucial for several reasons:

1. Value Communication: Onboarding is an opportunity to communicate the value proposition of the product clearly. It should demonstrate how the product meets the user's needs and solves their problems.

2. Habit Formation: A well-designed onboarding process can plant the seeds for habit formation by introducing users to the habit loop (cue-routine-reward) and encouraging repeat usage.

3. User Retention: A smooth onboarding experience can reduce user drop-off and increase retention. Users who understand the product's value are more likely to continue using it.

4. User Engagement: Engaging onboarding experiences capture users' attention and encourage them to explore the product further. It sets the stage for long-term engagement.

Principles for Successful Onboarding

1. Simplicity: Keep the onboarding process simple and intuitive. Avoid overwhelming users with too much information at once. Gradually introduce features and concepts to make it easy for users to follow.

2. Guided Progression: Guide users through the onboarding process with clear steps and instructions. Provide visual cues and tooltips to help users understand how to use the product effectively.

3. Value Demonstration: Demonstrate the product's value early on. Show users how the product solves their problem or fulfills their needs to capture their interest and motivation to continue.

4. Personalization: Tailor the onboarding experience to each user's preferences and goals. Use user data to provide relevant content and recommendations during the onboarding process.

5. Interactive and Engaging: Make the onboarding experience interactive and engaging. Use animations, interactive elements, and gamification to capture users' attention and keep them interested.

Strategies for Effective Onboarding

1. User Onboarding Flow: Design a clear and sequential onboarding flow that guides users through the product's key features and benefits. Break down the onboarding process into manageable steps to prevent information overload.

2. Onboarding Tutorials: Use interactive tutorials to introduce users to essential features and demonstrate how to use them. Interactive tutorials allow users to practice using the product in a safe environment.

3. Progressive Onboarding: Progressive onboarding gradually introduces users to more advanced features as they become more familiar with the product. This approach prevents overwhelming new users while offering more experienced users additional value.

4. In-App Guidance: Provide in-app guidance and tooltips to offer real-time assistance as users explore the product. In-app guidance helps users understand the context and purpose of each feature.

5. Welcome Emails: Send personalized welcome emails to new users that highlight the product's unique value proposition and provide links to relevant resources and guides.

6. Video Tutorials: Create video tutorials that showcase the product's key features and demonstrate how to perform common tasks. Video tutorials can be more engaging and easier to follow than written guides.

7. Gamified Onboarding: Gamify the onboarding process to make it enjoyable and rewarding for users. Use badges, rewards, and progress bars to encourage users to complete each step of the onboarding process.

Monitoring and Improving Onboarding

1. User Feedback: Collect user feedback on the onboarding experience through surveys, user interviews, or in-app feedback forms. Use this feedback to identify pain points and areas for improvement.

2. A/B Testing: Conduct A/B testing to compare different onboarding approaches and identify which methods are most effective in driving user engagement and retention.

3. Data Analysis: Analyze user data to understand how users progress through the onboarding process and identify drop-off points. Use this data to optimize the onboarding flow for better user retention.

4. Iterative Design: Onboarding is an iterative process, and continuous improvement is essential. Implement changes based on user feedback and data analysis to enhance the onboarding experience over time.

Conclusion

Onboarding is a critical phase in the user's journey, setting the stage for habit formation and long-term engagement with the product. By following the principles of simplicity, guided progression, value demonstration, personalization, and interactivity, product designers can create effective onboarding experiences that lead users from novice to habitual users.

Strategies such as user onboarding flows, tutorials, in-app guidance, welcome emails, video tutorials, and gamified onboarding can enhance the onboarding process and increase user retention. Monitoring and analyzing user feedback and data is essential for continuous improvement and optimization of the onboarding experience.

By prioritizing the onboarding process and investing in a seamless and engaging experience, product designers can foster habit formation, build user loyalty, and ensure users make a successful transition from novices to habitual users of the product.

16. Gamification and Habit Loops

Gamification is the incorporation of game-like elements into non-game contexts to engage users and drive desired behaviors. When combined with habit loops, gamification becomes a powerful tool for building habit-forming products. In this chapter, we explore the relationship between gamification and habit loops, the psychology behind their effectiveness, and how product designers can leverage this combination to create engaging and habit-forming experiences.

The Psychology of Gamification

Gamification taps into several psychological principles that make games engaging and enjoyable:

1. Intrinsic Motivation: Games often provide a sense of autonomy, competence, and relatedness, which fosters intrinsic motivation. Intrinsic motivation drives users to engage in an activity for its own sake, rather than for external rewards.

2. Progress and Mastery: Games offer clear goals and a sense of progression as players advance through levels or achieve milestones. The feeling of mastery and accomplishment keeps users engaged and motivated to continue playing.

3. Rewards and Feedback: Games provide immediate and tangible feedback through rewards, points, or badges, which reinforces desired behaviors and encourages repeat engagement.

4. Social Interaction: Multiplayer games and leaderboards foster a sense of social interaction and competition, motivating users to perform better and stay engaged.

The Habit Loop and Gamification

The habit loop (cue-routine-reward) shares similarities with game mechanics, making gamification and habit loops a natural fit:

1. Cue: In gamification, cues can be game elements that signal the start of a game-like experience, such as a progress bar or a notification for an upcoming challenge.

2. Routine: The routine in gamification is the gameplay itself, where users perform actions or complete tasks to progress through the game.

3. Reward: Game elements like points, badges, or virtual currency act as rewards in gamification, providing positive reinforcement for completing tasks and achieving goals.

The merging of the habit loop and gamification creates a powerful combination that leverages the psychological appeal of games to drive habit formation. As users engage in game-like activities repeatedly, habits are formed, and the desire to continue engaging with the product becomes more automatic and ingrained.

Designing Gamified Habit Loops

To create effective gamified habit loops, product designers should consider the following principles:

1. Clear Goals and Progression: Set clear goals and define a sense of progression for users to follow. Provide a visual representation of their progress, such as a progress bar or a level system.

2. Immediate Feedback: Offer immediate feedback to users when they complete tasks or achieve milestones. Use rewards like points or badges to reinforce positive behaviors.

3. Meaningful Rewards: Ensure that the rewards offered in the gamified experience are meaningful to users. Customizable rewards can enhance the feeling of autonomy and intrinsic motivation.

4. Social Elements: Incorporate social elements, such as leaderboards or collaborative challenges, to foster a sense of community and competition among users.

5. Replayability: Design tasks and challenges that are replayable and offer a sense of variety. This keeps users engaged and motivated to come back for more.

Case Study: Fitness Tracking Apps

Fitness tracking apps often use gamification and habit loops to encourage users to stay active and adopt healthy habits. These apps set daily step goals as clear objectives (cue), prompt users to walk or exercise regularly (routine) and reward users with badges or virtual rewards for achieving their fitness goals (reward). The continuous cycle of setting and achieving new goals fosters habit formation, making exercise a regular part of users' routines.

Balancing Gamification and Product Value

While gamification can be a powerful tool for habit formation, it is essential to strike a balance between game mechanics and the core value of the product.

The gamified elements should complement and enhance the product's purpose, rather than distracting users from it.

1. Align with User Goals: Ensure that the gamified elements align with users' goals and expectations. The game mechanics should support the overall value proposition of the product.

2. Avoid Overwhelming Users: Avoid overwhelming users with excessive gamification or complex game mechanics. Keep the experience simple, intuitive, and enjoyable.

3. Gradual Progression: Allow users to start with simple tasks and gradually introduce more complex challenges as they become more familiar with the gamified features.

Ethical Considerations in Gamification

Gamification can be a powerful motivator, but it also comes with ethical considerations:

1. Avoiding Manipulation: Avoid using gamification techniques to manipulate or coerce users into engaging with the product excessively. The focus should be on empowering users, not exploiting their vulnerabilities.

2. Transparent Design: Be transparent about the use of gamified elements and how they influence user behavior. Users should be aware of the purpose and consequences of engaging in gamified activities.

3. User Well-Being: Prioritize user well-being over maximizing engagement. Design gamified experiences that promote positive behaviors and support users' mental and physical health.

Conclusion

Gamification and habit loops are a dynamic duo that can transform user engagement and foster habit formation. By leveraging the psychological appeal of games and incorporating game-like elements into the habit loop, product designers can create engaging and habit-forming experiences.

Designing clear goals, providing immediate feedback, offering meaningful rewards, incorporating social elements, and ensuring replayability are key principles for effective gamified habit loops. Balancing gamification with the core value of the product and considering ethical considerations are essential for building habit-forming products that prioritize user well-being.

By merging play and routine, product designers can create habit-forming products that resonate with users, encourage positive behaviors, and enhance user satisfaction. Gamified habit loops have the power to captivate users and turn them into habitual users who keep coming back for more, ultimately leading to long-term success for the product.

17. Analyzing and Enhancing User Engagement

As product designers, it is essential to continuously analyze and optimize user engagement to build habit-forming products successfully. The Habit Loop Audit is a systematic process that allows product teams to examine the effectiveness of habit loops within their products and identify areas for improvement. In this chapter, we explore the importance of conducting a Habit Loop Audit, the key steps involved in the process, and how to use the findings to enhance user engagement and habit formation.

The Habit Loop: A Recap

The Habit Loop, comprising the cue, routine, and reward, serves as the foundation for habit formation. It is a cyclical process where cues trigger routines, leading to rewards that reinforce the behavior, ultimately making it more automatic and habitual.

1. Cue: The trigger or prompt that initiates a habitual behavior.

2. Routine: The actual behavior or action performed in response to the cue.

3. Reward: The positive reinforcement or benefit that follows the completion of the routine.

The Habit Loop is the backbone of habit-forming products, and understanding its effectiveness is crucial for driving user engagement and habit formation.

The Importance of the Habit Loop Audit

The Habit Loop Audit is a methodical evaluation of how well the Habit Loop functions within a product. It is designed to assess whether the cue, routine, and reward are optimally aligned to encourage habit formation and sustained user engagement.

The Habit Loop Audit provides several benefits:

1. Identifying Weak Points: By examining the Habit Loop, product teams can identify weak points where engagement and habit formation may be faltering.

2. Enhancing User Experience: Insights from the audit can lead to improvements in the user experience, making it more engaging and habit-forming.

3. Personalization: The Habit Loop Audit helps uncover opportunities for personalization, allowing product teams to tailor the experience to individual users' preferences and goals.

4. Iterative Design: The audit fosters an iterative design approach, encouraging continuous improvement and optimization of the product.

The Habit Loop Audit Process

1. Data Collection: Gather relevant user data, including user interactions, engagement metrics, and behavioral patterns. Utilize analytics tools, surveys, user interviews, and feedback to collect comprehensive data.

2. Define User Goals: Understand the goals and motivations of the target users. Define the desired behaviors and habits the product aims to promote.

3. Analyze User Behavior: Examine user behavior within the product. Track how users respond to cues, perform routines, and engage with rewards.

4. Identify Drop-Off Points: Identify drop-off points in the user journey where engagement decreases or users fail to complete the Habit Loop.

5. Assess User Feedback: Incorporate user feedback and sentiments about the Habit Loop. Gather insights into how users perceive and respond to the cues, routines, and rewards.

6. Evaluate Reward Relevance: Evaluate the relevance and appeal of the rewards provided within the Habit Loop. Ensure that the rewards align with user motivations and drive sustained engagement.

7. Review Personalization Opportunities: Assess opportunities for personalization within the Habit Loop. Consider how tailoring the experience to individual users' preferences can enhance engagement.

8. Cross-Functional Collaboration: Encourage collaboration between product designers, data analysts, user researchers, and other stakeholders to gain a comprehensive understanding of Habit Loop's effectiveness.

9. Benchmarking: Compare the product's Habit Loop with industry best practices and successful habit-forming products. Identify areas where the product can learn from others' successes.

Using Audit Findings to Enhance User Engagement

1. Optimize Cues: Based on the audit findings, refine the cues to make them more noticeable and effective. Clear, contextually relevant cues help trigger desired behaviors.

2. Streamline Routines: Simplify and streamline the routines within the Habit Loop to reduce friction and make the experience more seamless for users.

3. Enhance Rewards: Ensure that the rewards provided are genuinely rewarding and appealing to users. Consider offering a variety of rewards to cater to different user preferences.

4. A/B Testing: Conduct A/B testing to compare different versions of the Habit Loop and measure their impact on user engagement.

5. Personalization Strategies: Implement personalization strategies based on user preferences, behavior, and goals. Tailored experiences increase user motivation and commitment.

6. Gamification: Introduce gamification elements to make the Habit Loop more engaging and enjoyable. Gamification can enhance user motivation and encourage sustained engagement.

7. Iterative Improvements: Adopt an iterative design approach, continuously making improvements based on user feedback and data analysis.

8. Behavioral Nudges: Incorporate behavioral nudges within the Habit Loop to guide users toward desired behaviors and habits.

Conclusion

The Habit Loop Audit is a vital process for product teams seeking to build habit-forming products. By evaluating the effectiveness of the Habit Loop and identifying areas for improvement, product designers can enhance user engagement, foster habit formation, and drive long-term user loyalty.

Data collection, user feedback analysis, personalization, and cross-functional collaboration are critical components of the Habit Loop Audit. Using the audit findings to optimize cues, streamline routines, enhance rewards, and implement gamification ensures that the product remains engaging and habit-forming for its users.

The Habit Loop Audit is an ongoing process that supports iterative design and continuous improvement. By prioritizing the Habit Loop and conducting regular audits, product teams can build habit-forming products that create lasting user habits and contribute to the long-term success of the product.

18. Habit-Forming Marketing

Habit-forming marketing plays a crucial role in building and sustaining user engagement with habit-forming products. Effective marketing strategies can persuade users to adopt new habits, drive initial product adoption, and foster long-term retention. In this chapter, we explore the principles of habit-forming marketing, the psychology behind persuasive techniques, and strategies to retain users and build lasting habits.

Understanding Habit-Forming Marketing

Habit-forming marketing focuses on creating persuasive messaging and experiences that drive user behavior and encourage repeated product usage. It aims to build strong emotional connections between users and the product, making it a natural part of their daily routines.

The Psychology of Persuasion

Effective habit-forming marketing relies on psychological principles that influence user behavior:

1. Social Proof: The tendency to adopt behaviors based on the actions of others. Social proof can be demonstrated through testimonials, user reviews, and user-generated content.

2. Scarcity: The perception that a product or opportunity is limited or in high demand. Scarcity can trigger a fear of missing out (FOMO) and prompt users to take action.

3. Authority: The tendency to follow the advice or recommendations of perceived authorities or experts. Establishing the product's credibility and showcasing endorsements can influence user decisions.

4. Reciprocity: The inclination to return favors and gestures. Offering value upfront, such as free trials or exclusive content, can encourage users to reciprocate their engagement.

5. Cognitive Biases: Leveraging cognitive biases, such as the anchoring effect or the framing effect, can influence users' perceptions and decisions.

Persuasion Strategies for Habit Formation

1. Storytelling: Craft compelling narratives that resonate with users' aspirations and goals. Stories can create emotional connections and make the product's value more relatable.

2. Behavior Prompts: Use persuasive prompts that encourage desired behaviors and habits. For example, using action-oriented language or creating urgency with time-sensitive offers.

3. Personalization: Tailor marketing messages and experiences to individual user preferences and needs. Personalization increases the relevance and effectiveness of marketing efforts.

4. Engagement Triggers: Identify triggers that prompt users to engage with the product. Triggers can be external (e.g., push notifications) or internal (e.g., emotional states).

5. Referral Programs: Leverage social proof and reciprocity by implementing referral programs that incentivize users to invite others to the product.

6. Influencer Marketing: Collaborate with influencers and thought leaders who align with the product's values and target audience. Influencers can amplify brand awareness and credibility.

Retaining Users through Habit-Forming Marketing

1. Onboarding Nudges: Utilize nudges during the onboarding process to guide users towards forming habits. Nudges can remind users of their goals and encourage consistent product usage.

2. Feedback and Rewards: Provide immediate feedback and rewards for completing desired actions or hitting milestones. Positive reinforcement strengthens habit loops and encourages sustained engagement.

3. Gamified Experiences: Implement gamification elements in marketing campaigns to make the user experience more enjoyable and engaging.

4. Personalized Retention Campaigns: Create personalized retention campaigns based on user behavior and preferences. Tailored messages can re-engage users and encourage them to return to the product.

5. Targeted Re-Engagement: Identify inactive users and implement targeted re-engagement campaigns to bring them back to the product. Re-engagement can be achieved through special offers, content, or personalized incentives.

6. Continuous Communication: Maintain consistent communication with users to keep them informed about product updates, new features, and relevant content.

Building Long-Term Habits

1. Habit-Tracking Features: Incorporate habit-tracking features within the product. Progress tracking reinforces user commitment to their habits and encourages continued usage.

2. Habit-Streaks and Milestones: Celebrate users' habit-streaks and milestones to acknowledge their achievements and motivate further engagement.

3. Periodic Challenges: Introduce periodic challenges or events that align with users' goals and encourage them to stay engaged with the product.

4. Community Engagement: Foster a sense of community among users through forums, social media groups, or user-generated content. Community engagement enhances user loyalty and accountability.

5. Surveys and Feedback: Regularly collect user feedback to understand their evolving needs and expectations. Incorporate user input into product updates and improvements.

Ethical Considerations in Habit-Forming Marketing

1. Honesty and Transparency: Be honest and transparent in marketing communications. Avoid using manipulative tactics or making false promises.

2. User Well-Being: Prioritize user well-being over short-term gains. Marketing efforts should align with the product's value and contribute positively to users' lives.

3. Opt-Out Options: Provide clear opt-out options for users who wish to disengage from marketing communications.

Conclusion

Habit-forming marketing is a powerful tool for driving user engagement and fostering long-term habits. Understanding the psychology of persuasion and incorporating effective strategies can influence user behavior and encourage habitual product usage.

By leveraging social proof, scarcity, authority, reciprocity, and cognitive biases, product designers can create persuasive marketing campaigns that resonate with users. Tailored onboarding nudges, feedback and rewards, gamified experiences, and personalized retention campaigns can increase user retention and loyalty.

When using habit-forming marketing strategies, it is essential to consider ethical considerations, such as honesty, transparency, and user well-being. By prioritizing user satisfaction and building authentic emotional connections, product designers can create habit-forming products that not only hook users but also enrich their lives and promote positive behaviors.

19. Integrating Products into Daily Life

In today's digital age, users interact with a multitude of products and services daily. Building habit-forming products that stand out and become an integral part of users' lives requires more than just individual product design. Habit ecosystems involve creating a seamless and interconnected network of products and services that work together to fulfill users' needs and create a unified user experience. In this chapter, we explore the concept of habit ecosystems, the benefits they offer, and strategies for integrating products into users' daily lives.

Understanding Habit Ecosystems

A habit ecosystem is a network of interconnected products and services that work together to address various aspects of users' lives. Rather than focusing solely on individual products, habit ecosystems take a holistic approach to meet users' needs and foster habitual behaviors across different contexts and situations.

Key Components of Habit Ecosystems

1. Interconnectedness: Products within the ecosystem are interconnected and communicate with one another to provide a seamless user experience. This allows for the exchange of data and insights to personalize the user experience further.

2. Cross-Platform Integration: Habit ecosystems span multiple platforms and devices, enabling users to engage with products seamlessly across different channels.

3. Complementary Services: Products within the ecosystem complement one another, providing users with a comprehensive solution to their needs.

4. Personalization: Habit ecosystems leverage user data to personalize the user experience, offering tailored content, recommendations, and features.

5. Shared Habit Loops: Products within the ecosystem share common habit loops, reinforcing habitual behaviors and creating consistency in user engagement.

Benefits of Habit Ecosystems

1. Enhanced User Experience: By integrating products and services, habit ecosystems provide users with a cohesive and seamless experience that aligns with their preferences and goals.

2. Increased Engagement: Users are more likely to stay engaged when products within the ecosystem reinforce one another and encourage habit formation.

3. Cross-Selling and Upselling Opportunities: Habit ecosystems present opportunities for cross-selling and upselling, as users are more inclined to explore related products within the ecosystem.

4. Improved User Retention: A holistic user experience fosters user loyalty and reduces the likelihood of users seeking alternatives outside the ecosystem.

5. Data Synergy: Data exchange and integration between products offer valuable insights that can drive personalization and further enhance the user experience.

Strategies for Building Habit Ecosystems

1. Identify User Needs and Goals: Understand the diverse needs and goals of your target audience to identify areas where the ecosystem can add value and address user pain points.

2. Seamless User Onboarding: Create a seamless onboarding process for users as they engage with different products within the ecosystem. Shared user data can facilitate a personalized onboarding experience.

3. Cross-Platform Integration: Ensure that products within the ecosystem are accessible across various platforms and devices. This enables users to transition seamlessly between different touchpoints.

4. Shared Habit Loops: Identify common habit loops that can be shared across products to reinforce desired behaviors and encourage habitual engagement.

5. Interconnected Notifications: Use notifications and alerts to keep users informed about relevant updates and activities across the ecosystem.

6. Personalization and Data Sharing: Leverage user data to personalize the user experience across products within the ecosystem. Ensure that data sharing is transparent and aligns with user consent.

Case Study: Habit Ecosystem of a Health and Fitness App

A health and fitness app can form a habit ecosystem by integrating complementary products and services:

1. Core Health App: The central health and fitness app serves as the core of the ecosystem, providing users with personalized fitness plans, tracking their activities, and offering nutrition guidance.

2. Wearable Devices: Integrate wearable devices like fitness trackers and smartwatches to collect data on users' daily activities, sleep patterns, and heart rates.

3. Meal Planning Service: Incorporate a meal planning service that syncs with the health app, offering personalized meal suggestions based on users' fitness goals and nutritional preferences.

4. Online Community: Create an online community platform where users can connect, share their fitness achievements, and seek support from like-minded individuals.

5. E-Commerce Platform: Offer an e-commerce platform within the app that sells health supplements, fitness gear, and other products related to users' health and fitness goals.

6. Virtual Coaching: Provide virtual coaching sessions or personalized workout videos to guide users through their fitness journey.

Data Privacy and Security Considerations

Building habit ecosystems involves data exchange and integration between products. Product designers must prioritize data privacy and security to ensure that user information is protected and used responsibly. Implement clear data-sharing policies and obtain user consent for data usage within the ecosystem.

Conclusion

Habit ecosystems are a powerful approach to building habit-forming products that integrate seamlessly into users' daily lives. By creating interconnected products and services that complement one another, habit ecosystems enhance the user experience, increase engagement, and foster long-term user retention.

Identifying user needs and goals, ensuring cross-platform integration, leveraging shared habit loops, and personalizing the user experience are essential strategies for building effective habit ecosystems. While the benefits of habit ecosystems are numerous, it is essential to prioritize data privacy and security to build trust with users and ensure responsible data usage.

By adopting a holistic approach to product design and creating interconnected experiences, product designers can build habit-forming products that become an indispensable part of users' daily routines and contribute positively to their lives. Habit ecosystems are not just about individual products; they represent a new paradigm for creating value and fostering lasting user habits in an interconnected digital world.

20. The Role of Emotions in Habit Building

Triggers play a pivotal role in habit formation and the success of habit-forming products. Triggers are cues or stimuli that prompt users to engage in certain behaviors or routines. Emotions are powerful triggers that can significantly influence user behavior and drive habitual product usage. In this chapter, we explore the impact of emotions as triggers in habit formation, the psychology behind emotional triggers, and strategies for designing habit-forming products that leverage emotions to drive user engagement.

The Role of Emotions in Habit Formation

Emotions play a fundamental role in human decision-making and behavior. They have the power to influence how users perceive and interact with products, driving them to form habits around products that evoke strong emotional responses.

1. Emotional Resonance: Products that evoke positive emotions such as joy, excitement, or delight create an emotional resonance with users. When users associate positive emotions with a product, they are more likely to engage with it repeatedly.

2. Emotional Connection: Products that create a deep emotional connection with users become more than just tools; they become an integral part of users' lives. An emotional bond fosters habitual usage as users seek to replicate the positive emotional experience.

3. Emotional Memory: Emotional experiences are more memorable than neutral ones. Products that trigger strong emotions are likely to stay top-of-mind for users, leading to continued usage.

4. Emotional Regulation: Users may turn to habit-forming products to regulate their emotions. Products that offer a sense of comfort, stress relief, or emotional support can become go-to solutions for emotional regulation.

The Psychology of Emotional Triggers

Understanding the psychology behind emotional triggers is essential for designing products that evoke the desired emotional responses and foster habit formation.

1. Emotional Contagion: Humans are highly susceptible to "emotional contagion," where the emotions of others influence their emotional states.

Products that showcase positive emotions in user interactions can trigger similar positive emotions in users.

2. Emotional Arousal: Emotionally arousing content captures users' attention and enhances memory retention. Arousing content increases the likelihood of users engaging with the product repeatedly.

3. Emotional Reward: Positive emotions act as intrinsic rewards that reinforce user behavior. When users associate positive emotions with product usage, they are motivated to repeat the behavior to experience the emotional reward again.

Designing for Emotional Triggers

1. Empathy-Driven Design: Understand the emotional needs and pain points of your target audience through user research. The empathetic design addresses users' emotional challenges and creates emotionally resonant experiences.

2. Emotional Storytelling: Craft narratives and user experiences that evoke emotions and resonate with users' aspirations. Emotional storytelling helps create a deeper emotional connection between users and the product.

3. Emotional Design Elements: Incorporate emotional design elements such as colors, imagery, and animations that evoke specific emotions and set the tone for the user experience.

4. Emotional Language: Use language that speaks to users' emotions and addresses their desires and fears. The use of emotional language can heighten engagement and emotional resonance.

5. Personalization for Emotional Impact: Personalize the user experience to evoke emotions that align with individual user preferences and goals. Personalized content enhances emotional relevance.

Case Study: Emotional Triggers in Social Media Apps

Social media apps are known for their ability to trigger strong emotions in users:

1. Emotional Contagion: Platforms like Facebook and Instagram showcase users' positive experiences, creating emotional contagion as users feel compelled to share their own positive moments.

2. Emotional Storytelling: Snapchat's "Stories" feature allows users to share narratives of their day, creating emotional connections with followers and eliciting emotional responses from viewers.

3. Emotional Design: Social media platforms use vibrant colors, playful animations, and emotive icons to evoke positive emotions and create an engaging user interface.

4. Emotional Language: Apps like Twitter and TikTok encourage users to express themselves emotionally through short, impactful messages or videos.

Ethical Considerations in Emotional Trigger Design

1. Respectful Emotional Triggers: Design emotional triggers that respect users' emotions and well-being. Avoid using negative emotions to manipulate or coerce user behavior.

2. Emotional Regulation: Be mindful of how products may be used for emotional regulation, ensuring that the product fosters healthy habits rather than dependence.

3. Transparency: Be transparent about the emotional triggers used in the product design. Users should be aware of how emotions are leveraged to drive engagement.

Conclusion

Emotional triggers are powerful tools for driving user engagement and habit formation. By understanding the role of emotions in habit-building and leveraging psychological principles, product designers can create emotionally resonant experiences that foster lasting user habits.

Empathetic design, emotional storytelling, emotional design elements, emotional language, and personalization are essential strategies for designing emotionally engaging products.

When leveraging emotional triggers, it is crucial to consider ethical considerations, respecting users' emotions and well-being. By prioritizing the creation of positive emotional experiences, product designers can build habit-forming products that not only hook users but also enrich their lives and foster a genuine emotional connection with the product. Emotional triggers are a potent force for building meaningful and sustainable user habits in the increasingly emotion-driven digital landscape.

21. Cultivating User Behavior Change

The Hooked Mindset is a powerful concept that revolves around understanding user psychology and behavior to cultivate lasting behavior change. Habit-forming products aim to create a seamless and addictive user experience, but achieving true habit formation requires more than just a clever product design. In this chapter, we delve into the Hooked Mindset, the psychological principles that underpin it, and strategies for cultivating user behavior change to build habit-forming products that stand the test of time.

Understanding the Hooked Mindset

The Hooked Mindset is about empowering users to take charge of their behaviors and form positive habits. It involves tapping into users' motivations, emotions, and aspirations to create products that become an integral part of their lives.

Key Principles of the Hooked Mindset

1. User-Centricity: The Hooked Mindset puts users at the center of product design, focusing on meeting their needs, desires, and goals.

2. Behavior Analysis: It involves a deep understanding of user behavior and the factors that drive behavior change.

3. Empowerment: The Hooked Mindset empowers users to take positive actions and make meaningful changes in their lives.

4. Emotional Resonance: It leverages emotional triggers to foster emotional connections with the product, increasing user engagement and habit formation.

5. Iterative Improvement: The Hooked Mindset embraces an iterative approach to product design, continuously refining and optimizing the user experience based on user feedback and data.

The Psychology of Behavior Change

To cultivate behavior change and build habit-forming products, product designers need to understand the psychological principles that drive human behavior:

1. Motivation: Understanding user motivations and aligning the product with those motivations is crucial for driving behavior change.

2. Habit Loops: Habit loops, consisting of cues, routines, and rewards, play a central role in forming habits and encouraging repeated product usage.

3. Social Influence: Humans are highly influenced by social factors, including social proof, peer pressure, and the desire for social acceptance.

4. Cognitive Biases: Leveraging cognitive biases, such as the anchoring effect or loss aversion, can influence decision-making and behavior.

5. Intrinsic vs. Extrinsic Motivation: Cultivating intrinsic motivation, where users engage with the product for its inherent value, is more sustainable than relying solely on extrinsic rewards.

Strategies for Cultivating Behavior Change

1. Clear Goal Setting: Encourage users to set clear, achievable goals within the product. Goal setting enhances motivation and provides a sense of progress.

2. Small Wins and Streaks: Celebrate users' small wins and habit streaks to reinforce positive behaviors and build momentum.

3. Social Reinforcement: Incorporate social elements that allow users to share their progress, achievements, and challenges with their social network.

4. Personalized Recommendations: Offer personalized recommendations and content that align with users' goals and preferences.

5. Feedback and Rewards: Provide immediate feedback and meaningful rewards for completing desired actions or hitting milestones.

6. Behavior Nudges: Incorporate behavior nudges to gently guide users toward desired behaviors and actions.

Case Study: Fitness App and the Hooked Mindset

A fitness app can embrace the Hooked Mindset to cultivate user behavior change:

1. User-Centric Design: The app's interface is intuitive and tailored to users' fitness goals, making it easy for them to track progress and engage with personalized workouts.

2. Goal Setting: The app encourages users to set specific fitness goals, such as running a certain distance or completing a set number of workouts per week.

3. Social Reinforcement: Users can share their achievements and progress with friends and followers, fostering a sense of community and accountability.

4. Feedback and Rewards: The app provides real-time feedback during workouts and rewards users with badges for hitting milestones or maintaining a consistent workout routine.

Ethical Considerations in Behavior Change

When cultivating behavior change, it is essential to consider ethical implications:

1. Informed Consent: Ensure that users are aware of the behavior change aspects of the product and provide clear information on data usage and privacy.

2. User Well-Being: Prioritize user well-being over maximizing engagement. Avoid manipulating users into forming habits that may not be in their best interest.

3. Transparent Design: Be transparent about the product's intentions and the strategies used to cultivate behavior change.

Conclusion

The Hooked Mindset is a transformative approach to building habit-forming products that cultivate user behavior change. By understanding the psychological principles that underpin human behavior, product designers can create products that resonate with users on a deep emotional level and foster positive habits.

User-centric design, goal setting, social reinforcement, personalized recommendations, feedback and rewards, and behavior nudges are essential strategies for cultivating behavior change and building habit-forming products. When implementing the Hooked Mindset, it is vital to prioritize user well-being and maintain ethical practices. By empowering users to make positive changes in their lives, habit-forming products can become more than just tools; they can become catalysts for lasting behavior change and personal growth. The Hooked Mindset represents a paradigm shift in product design—one that embraces empathy, motivation, and human-centric solutions to create products that users truly value and integrate into their daily lives.

22. The Power of Habitual Engagement

In the pursuit of building habit-forming products, user experience (UX) is often a primary focus for product designers. However, achieving true habit formation goes beyond merely providing a seamless and delightful user experience. Habitual engagement is the key to creating products that become ingrained in users' daily lives and foster lasting habits. In this chapter, we explore the concept of habitual engagement, its significance in building habit-forming products, and strategies for cultivating long-term user habits.

Understanding Habitual Engagement

Habitual engagement refers to the consistent and automatic use of a product, driven by habit rather than conscious decision-making. When users form habits around a product, it becomes an integral part of their routines, leading to sustained engagement over time.

Key Characteristics of Habitual Engagement

1. Autopilot Behavior: Users engage with the product on autopilot, without consciously thinking about it. Habitual engagement reduces cognitive effort and friction in product usage.

2. Emotional Resonance: Products that foster emotional connections with users are more likely to cultivate habitual engagement. Emotional resonance creates a positive association with the product.

3. User Goals Alignment: Habitually engaging products align with users' goals and aspirations, providing value that reinforces the desired behaviors.

4. Reduced Decision Fatigue: Habitual engagement minimizes decision fatigue, as users no longer need to deliberate on whether to use the product.

The Significance of Habitual Engagement

1. Sustained User Retention: Habitual engagement leads to sustained user retention and loyalty. Users who have formed habits around a product are less likely to churn.

2. Reduced Competitor Threat: Habitual engagement creates a competitive advantage, as users are less likely to switch to alternatives.

3. User Advocacy: Habitually engaged users are more likely to become brand advocates and refer others to the product.

4. Long-Term Business Success: Building habitual engagement fosters a foundation for long-term business success and growth.

Strategies for Cultivating Habitual Engagement

1. Habit Loop Optimization: Analyze the Habit Loop within the product and optimize cues, routines, and rewards to encourage habitual engagement.

2. Personalization and Relevance: Personalize the user experience to make it more relevant and aligned with individual user goals.

3. Habit-Building Onboarding: Design onboarding experiences that nudge users toward forming habits from the outset.

4. Emotional Resonance: Create emotionally resonant experiences that foster positive associations with the product.

5. Continuous Value Delivery: Consistently deliver value to users to reinforce habitual engagement. Regular updates and new features keep users coming back.

6. Behavioral Nudges: Incorporate behavioral nudges to encourage habitual engagement and support users' long-term goals.

Case Study: Social Media Platform and Habitual Engagement

A social media platform can cultivate habitual engagement through various strategies:

1. Habit Loop Optimization: The platform optimizes the Habit Loop by providing engaging cues (notifications, new content), routines (scrolling, commenting), and rewards (likes, shares).

2. Personalization: The platform uses algorithms to personalize users' feeds, showing content relevant to their interests and connections.

3. Emotional Resonance: The platform encourages emotional connections through social interactions, facilitating positive experiences with friends and family.

4. Continuous Value Delivery: The platform introduces new features, filters, and interactive elements to keep users engaged and entertained.

Ethical Considerations in Habitual Engagement

1. Transparency: Be transparent about the mechanisms used to foster habitual engagement and respect users' autonomy.

2. User Well-Being: Prioritize user well-being over maximizing engagement. Avoid exploiting psychological vulnerabilities for prolonged engagement.

3. Empowering Users: Empower users to manage their engagement and set healthy boundaries.

Conclusion

Beyond user experience lies the realm of habitual engagement—the ultimate goal for building habit-forming products. By understanding the significance of habitual engagement and the factors that drive it, product designers can create products that become ingrained in users' daily routines and foster lasting habits. Strategies such as Habit Loop optimization, personalization, habit-building onboarding, emotional resonance, continuous value delivery, and behavioral nudges are essential for cultivating habitual engagement.

In the pursuit of habitual engagement, it is essential to prioritize ethical considerations, such as transparency, user well-being, and empowering users to control their engagement. By building products that genuinely resonate with users and fulfill their goals, habit-forming products can become valuable tools that enhance users' lives and create positive, long-term relationships with their audience. Habitual engagement represents the pinnacle of product design—a harmonious integration of user needs and behavior to cultivate lasting user habits and drive long-term business success.

23. The Future of Habit-Forming Products

The landscape of habit-forming products is constantly evolving, driven by advancements in technology, changing user behaviors, and new challenges. As we look toward the future, product designers must adapt and innovate to continue building habit-forming products that resonate with users and stand the test of time. In this chapter, we explore the future of habit-forming products, emerging innovations, potential challenges, and strategies to navigate this ever-evolving landscape.

Emerging Innovations in Habit-Forming Products

1. Artificial Intelligence and Machine Learning: Advancements in AI and machine learning offer opportunities for personalized user experiences. AI-powered recommendation systems can better understand user preferences and behavior, leading to more effective habit-building strategies.

2. Voice Interfaces and Natural Language Processing: Voice interfaces and NLP enable more seamless and intuitive interactions with products, making it easier for users to engage with them habitually.

3. Virtual and Augmented Reality: VR and AR open up new possibilities for immersive experiences, transforming how users interact with products and potentially fostering deeper emotional connections.

4. Internet of Things (IoT): IoT devices create interconnected ecosystems that offer continuous and contextually relevant engagement, contributing to habitual product usage.

5. Neurotechnology: Advancements in neurotechnology may allow for deeper insights into user behavior and emotional responses, enhancing habit-forming strategies.

6. Gamification and Serious Games: Gamification elements and serious games can make habit-forming products more enjoyable and engaging, increasing user motivation and habit formation.

The Challenge of Ethical Design

As habit-forming products become more sophisticated, ethical considerations become even more critical. Designers must grapple with challenges related to privacy, data security, user well-being, and potential addiction. Addressing these challenges requires a commitment to responsible design practices and user-centric decision-making.

1. Data Privacy and Security: As habit-forming products collect vast amounts of user data, ensuring data privacy and security is paramount to building trust with users.

2. User Well-Being: Designers must balance the pursuit of engagement with user well-being, avoiding tactics that exploit vulnerabilities or lead to unhealthy usage patterns.

3. Addiction and Dependency: Addressing addiction and dependency concerns involves building mechanisms for user control, such as setting usage limits or offering support for those seeking to reduce usage.

Strategies for Ethical Design

1. Transparent Design: Be transparent about data usage, collection, and product intentions. Users should understand how their data is used and what to expect from the product.

2. Empowerment and User Control: Give users the tools and information to control their engagement with the product. This includes setting usage limits, providing user settings, and educating users about healthy usage patterns.

3. User Feedback and Testing: Gather user feedback and conduct usability testing to understand the impact of the product on user well-being and iterate based on user insights.

4. Responsible Marketing: Avoid manipulative or misleading marketing tactics that encourage excessive usage or exploit users' emotions.

Looking Ahead: Designing for Positive Impact

1. Purposeful Habit Formation: Design habit-forming products with a clear purpose that aligns with users' goals and contributes positively to their lives.

2. Digital Well-Being: Consider the impact of the product on users' digital well-being and aim to enhance, rather than hinder, their overall well-being.

3. Sustainable Engagement: Prioritize sustainable engagement over short-term gains, ensuring that users continue to find value in the product over time.

4. Positive Behavioral Change: Focus on cultivating positive behavioral changes and habits that promote personal growth and empowerment.

Conclusion

The future of habit-forming products is full of promise, with emerging innovations offering exciting opportunities for personalized and immersive user experiences. However, this future also presents challenges related to ethical design and responsible usage. As product designers, it is our responsibility to navigate this evolving landscape with empathy, transparency, and user-centricity.

By embracing emerging technologies, remaining vigilant about ethical considerations, and designing for positive impact, we can build habit-forming products that enrich users' lives and foster lasting, meaningful habits. The future of habit-forming products is not just about building addictive experiences; it's about using design as a force for good—a means of empowering users, supporting their well-being, and creating products that genuinely add value to their lives.

24. Building Lasting Habits

In the pursuit of building habit-forming products, the ultimate goal is to create experiences that go beyond being merely "sticky" or addictive. Truly unforgettable products are those that become ingrained in users' lives, foster lasting habits, and evoke positive emotions and memories. In this chapter, we explore the journey from creating sticky products to building unforgettable ones, the key ingredients for lasting habit formation, and strategies to create products that leave a lasting impact on users.

Moving Beyond Stickiness: The Quest for Unforgettable Products
Sticky products are those that temporarily capture users' attention and keep them engaged for short bursts of time. While sticky products can be effective for immediate engagement, they may not necessarily lead to long-term behavior change or habit formation. The transition from sticky to unforgettable involves creating a more profound and lasting impact on users' lives.

Key Ingredients for Lasting Habit Formation
1. Meaningful Purpose: Unforgettable products are built with a clear and meaningful purpose that resonates with users' needs and aspirations. The product serves as a means of achieving their goals and enriching their lives.
2. Emotional Connection: Building emotional connections with users fosters a sense of attachment and loyalty. Unforgettable products evoke positive emotions, creating a lasting impact on users' memories and experiences.
3. Empowering User Journey: Unforgettable products empower users to take control of their behaviors and accomplish their objectives. They support users' growth and personal development.
4. Positive Reinforcement: The use of positive reinforcement, such as rewards, achievements, and progress tracking, encourages users to continue engaging with the product and reinforces positive habits.

Strategies for Building Unforgettable Products
1. Human-Centric Design: Center product design around the needs, goals, and emotions of users. Understand their aspirations and challenges to build products that truly resonate.

2. Emotional Storytelling: Craft narratives and experiences that elicit emotions and forge a deeper connection with users. Stories are a powerful tool for leaving a lasting impact.

3. Delightful Moments: Create delightful moments within the product that surprise and bring joy to users. Small gestures and interactions can have a significant impact on user experiences.

4. Personalization and Customization: Offer personalized experiences that cater to individual preferences and aspirations. Personalization enhances the feeling of being understood and valued.

5. Long-Term Value: Design products that provide enduring value to users, supporting their long-term goals and fostering continued engagement.

6. Ethical Considerations: Prioritize user well-being and adhere to ethical design practices. Avoid tactics that exploit psychological vulnerabilities or lead to unhealthy behaviors.

Case Study: Meditation App and Unforgettable Experiences

A meditation app can aim to be unforgettable by:

1. Meaningful Purpose: The app has a clear purpose of helping users find inner peace and mindfulness amid their busy lives.

2. Emotional Connection: The app creates emotional connections through guided meditation sessions that evoke tranquility and positive emotions.

3. Empowering User Journey: The app empowers users to cultivate a consistent meditation practice, offering personalized recommendations and progress tracking.

4. Positive Reinforcement: Users receive achievements and rewards for reaching meditation milestones, encouraging ongoing engagement.

Beyond Habit Formation: Creating User Advocates

Unforgettable products not only form habits but also create user advocates—loyal users who become enthusiastic brand ambassadors and recommend the product to others. User advocates are invaluable assets for product growth and success.

Strategies for Creating User Advocates:

1. Exceptional Customer Support: Provide excellent customer support and promptly address user inquiries or concerns.

2. Rewarding Loyalty: Offer exclusive benefits and rewards to loyal users to reinforce their commitment to the product.

3. Cultivating Community: Build a sense of community around the product, where users can connect, share experiences, and support one another.

4. Encouraging Word-of-Mouth: Facilitate word-of-mouth marketing by encouraging users to share their positive experiences with others.

5. Continuous Improvement: Consistently improve the product based on user feedback to demonstrate a commitment to user satisfaction.

Conclusion

The journey from building sticky products to creating unforgettable ones requires a deep understanding of user needs, emotions, and motivations. By focusing on meaningful purpose, emotional connection, empowering user journeys, and positive reinforcement, product designers can build products that go beyond immediate engagement and foster lasting habits.

Unforgettable products leave a lasting impact on users' lives, creating emotional connections and becoming indispensable parts of their daily routines. The transition from stickiness to unforgettable experiences is not just about building a product—it is about building a relationship with users, supporting their growth, and leaving a positive mark on their lives.

By prioritizing ethical considerations and cultivating user advocates, unforgettable products can become beacons of positive change, empowering users to achieve their goals and transforming their lives in meaningful ways. In the pursuit of creating unforgettable products, designers have the opportunity to make a lasting impact on individuals and society as a whole, leaving a legacy that goes far beyond mere engagement metrics.

25. Community and Habit Formation

Humans are social beings, and our interactions with others play a significant role in shaping our behaviors and habits. Social connections and communities have a profound impact on habit formation and the success of habit-forming products. In this chapter, we explore the power of the social element in fostering habit formation, the psychology behind social influences, and strategies for building thriving communities that drive long-term user engagement.

The Influence of Social Connections on Habit Formation

1. Social Proof: Social proof is the tendency to imitate the behaviors and choices of others when making decisions. When users see their peers engaging with a product or forming positive habits, they are more likely to follow suit.

2. Social Identity: Social identity theory posits that individuals derive a part of their self-concept from the groups they belong to. Being part of a community that promotes positive behaviors can strengthen users' commitment to forming similar habits.

3. Accountability: In a community, users feel accountable to their peers, creating a sense of responsibility to maintain positive habits and progress toward their goals.

4. Emotional Support: Social connections provide emotional support and encouragement, fostering resilience in the face of challenges and setbacks in habit formation.

Building Thriving Communities for Habit Formation

1. Facilitating Interaction: Design product features that facilitate user interaction and communication within the community. This can include chat functionalities, forums, or shared progress tracking.

2. Encouraging Collaboration: Encourage users to collaborate on challenges or projects, promoting a sense of teamwork and mutual support.

3. User-Generated Content: Allow users to contribute user-generated content, such as success stories, tips, or motivational posts. User-generated content strengthens the sense of community ownership.

4. Community Leaders and Moderators: Appoint community leaders or moderators who can guide discussions, resolve conflicts, and maintain a positive and inclusive atmosphere.

5. Events and Challenges: Organize events, challenges, or competitions within the community to keep users engaged and motivated.

The Role of Social Gamification

Social gamification is the integration of game elements with social interactions. By combining the power of social connections with game mechanics, social gamification can significantly enhance habit formation and community engagement.

1. Points, Badges, and Leaderboards: Implement points, badges, and leaderboards to recognize users' achievements and foster healthy competition within the community.

2. Team-Based Challenges: Organize team-based challenges where users work together to achieve common goals, strengthening the sense of camaraderie.

3. Virtual Rewards and Prizes: Offer virtual rewards or prizes to users who achieve certain milestones or actively contribute to the community.

Case Study: Fitness App and Social Gamification

A fitness app can leverage social gamification to enhance habit formation:

1. Social Leaderboards: The app features leaderboards where users can see their progress compared to others, encouraging friendly competition and motivation.

2. Team Challenges: Users can join teams and participate in challenges, where team members support and motivate each other to achieve their fitness goals.

3. Virtual Rewards: The app rewards users with virtual medals or trophies for reaching specific milestones, providing a sense of accomplishment and recognition.

The Dark Side of Social Influence

While social influence can be a powerful tool for habit formation, there are potential downsides and ethical concerns that product designers must consider:

1. Negative Peer Pressure: Social influence can lead to negative behaviors or habits if users are influenced by peers engaging in unhealthy activities.

2. Social Comparison: Constant social comparison can lead to feelings of inadequacy and decrease motivation if users perceive themselves as falling short compared to others.

3. Privacy Concerns: Communities that encourage sharing may raise privacy concerns if users feel uncomfortable sharing personal information.

Addressing Ethical Concerns in Social Communities

1. User Consent and Privacy: Obtain explicit user consent for sharing information within the community, and allow users to control the visibility of their data.

2. Positive Social Norms: Promote positive social norms within the community, focusing on healthy behaviors and mutual support.

3. Mindful Social Comparison: Encourage mindful social comparison, where users use others' progress as inspiration rather than a basis for self-worth.

Conclusion

The social element is a powerful driver of habit formation and long-term user engagement. Building thriving communities that foster positive behaviors and mutual support can transform habit-forming products into platforms that promote personal growth and empowerment.

Social gamification adds an extra layer of motivation and engagement, amplifying the impact of social connections on habit formation.

However, product designers must also be mindful of potential ethical concerns, such as negative peer pressure and privacy issues. By addressing these concerns and prioritizing user well-being, social communities can become powerful catalysts for building lasting habits and transforming users' lives. In harnessing the social element, habit-forming products have the potential to go beyond mere tools—they can become vehicles for positive change and a force for creating a more connected and supportive world.

26. Applying Brain Science to Product Development

Neurodesign is a revolutionary approach to product development that leverages insights from brain science to create products that resonate deeply with users and drive habit formation. Understanding how the brain processes information, emotions, and decision-making can significantly influence product design, user experience, and engagement. In this chapter, we explore the concept of neuro design, key principles of brain science in product development, and strategies for applying neuro design to build habit-forming products.

Understanding the Neuroscience of User Behavior

1. The Triune Brain Model: The triune brain model posits that the human brain comprises three distinct layers: the reptilian brain (responsible for basic survival instincts), the limbic system (associated with emotions and memory), and the neocortex (responsible for higher-order thinking and decision-making). Understanding how these brain regions interact can inform product design that appeals to different aspects of human behavior.

2. Emotion and Memory: Emotional experiences are more likely to be remembered by the brain. Products that evoke positive emotions are more likely to create lasting memories and encourage repeated usage.

3. The Dopamine System: Dopamine is a neurotransmitter associated with pleasure and reward. Habit-forming products often trigger the release of dopamine, reinforcing positive behaviors.

4. Cognitive Biases: Cognitive biases are inherent tendencies in human thinking that influence decision-making. By understanding these biases, product designers can create experiences that align with users' mental shortcuts.

Applying Neuroscience to Product Design

1. Emotional Design: Design products that elicit positive emotions through aesthetics, color schemes, and user interactions. The emotional design creates a memorable and enjoyable user experience.

2. Behavioral Nudges: Incorporate behavioral nudges that align with cognitive biases to guide users toward desired behaviors and actions.

3. Personalization: Leverage user data to personalize the product experience, catering to individual preferences and emotional triggers.

4. Microinteractions: Microinteractions are subtle, delightful interactions that contribute to a positive user experience. Pay attention to the details that evoke positive emotions.

Case Study: Social Media Platform and Emotional Design

A social media platform can apply emotional design principles:

1. User-Centric Visuals: The platform uses visually appealing and emotionally resonant visuals that evoke positive feelings.

2. Emotional Reactions: The platform allows users to express a range of emotions (like, love, laughter, etc.) to enrich emotional interactions.

3. Personalized Content: The content algorithm is designed to personalize users' feeds, showing posts that align with their interests and preferences.

Ethical Considerations in Neuro Design

While neurodesign can enhance user engagement, it also raises ethical considerations related to privacy, data usage, and psychological manipulation. Product designers must strike a balance between creating compelling experiences and safeguarding user well-being.

1. Transparency: Be transparent about data usage, privacy practices, and the mechanisms employed to influence user behavior.

2. User Consent: Obtain explicit user consent for collecting and using their data for personalization and behavioral nudging.

3. User Well-Being: Prioritize user well-being over maximizing engagement. Avoid manipulative tactics that exploit psychological vulnerabilities.

The Future of Neurodesign and Brain-Computer Interfaces

The future of neurodesign holds tremendous potential for building even more immersive and personalized experiences. Brain-computer interfaces (BCIs) could revolutionize how users interact with products by directly tapping into their brain signals.

1. Brainwave Tracking: BCIs can track users' brainwaves to measure emotional responses and engagement levels.

2. Neuroadaptive Systems: Neuroadaptive systems can dynamically adjust product experiences based on users' real-time brain activity, further enhancing personalization.

3. Ethical Considerations: The integration of BCIs in products raises important ethical concerns, such as data privacy and user consent.

Conclusion

Neurodesign represents a paradigm shift in product development, as it harnesses the power of brain science to create products that deeply resonate with users and drive lasting habit formation. By understanding the neuroscience of user behavior, emotional design, cognitive biases, and the ethical implications of neuro design, product designers can build habit-forming products that enrich users' lives while respecting their well-being.

The future of neurodesign and brain-computer interfaces holds the potential to create even more immersive and personalized experiences. However, product designers must remain mindful of ethical considerations and prioritize user consent, privacy, and well-being. In the pursuit of neurodesign, product designers have the opportunity to create transformative experiences that go beyond traditional user engagement, fostering deep connections and enriching users' lives in profound ways.

27. Responsibility in Product Design

As product designers, the power to influence user behavior comes with great responsibility. Persuasion techniques, when used ethically, can help create engaging and habit-forming products. However, there is a fine line between responsible persuasion and manipulative practices that exploit human psychology. In this chapter, we delve into the ethics of persuasion in product design, the potential risks of unethical practices, and strategies for maintaining ethical standards while building habit-forming products.

Understanding Ethical Persuasion

Ethical persuasion aims to guide users towards behaviors that align with their best interests and goals, without coercion or deceit. It involves designing products that provide genuine value and positive experiences to users.

Key Principles of Ethical Persuasion

1. Transparency: Be transparent about the intentions and mechanisms used to influence user behavior. Users should have a clear understanding of the product's purpose and potential impact on their habits.

2. User Empowerment: Empower users to make informed decisions and control their engagement with the product. Avoid manipulative tactics that limit user agency.

3. User Well-Being: Prioritize user well-being and avoid tactics that exploit psychological vulnerabilities or lead to addictive behaviors.

4. Long-Term Value: Design products that deliver long-term value and support users' goals, rather than focusing solely on short-term engagement metrics.

The Dark Side of Unethical Persuasion

Unethical persuasion can have detrimental effects on users' well-being and create a negative impact on society. Some of the risks associated with unethical practices in product design include:

1. Addiction and Dependency: Unethical products can foster addictive behaviors, leading to excessive usage and dependency on the product.

2. Mental Health Impacts: Manipulative tactics can negatively impact users' mental health, leading to increased stress, anxiety, and feelings of inadequacy.

3. Privacy and Data Exploitation: Unethical products may exploit user data and violate privacy rights, eroding trust between users and the product.

4. Social Impacts: Unethical persuasion can lead to harmful social dynamics, such as cyberbullying, misinformation spread, and toxic online environments.

Strategies for Ethical Product Design

1. User-Centric Approach: Design products with a user-centric focus, prioritizing user needs, goals, and well-being.

2. Informed Consent: Obtain explicit user consent for data collection, personalization, and behavioral nudging.

3. User Privacy: Respect user privacy rights and implement robust data protection measures.

4. Empowering User Settings: Provide users with settings and controls to manage their engagement, such as setting usage limits and turning off certain features.

5. Ethical Guidelines: Establish clear ethical guidelines for product design and ensure all team members understand and adhere to them.

Case Study: Social Media Platform and Ethical Design

An ethical social media platform can implement the following practices:

1. Time Management Features: The platform provides features that help users manage their time spent on the platform, such as setting daily usage reminders.

2. User Empowerment: Users have control over the visibility of their content and can opt out of certain types of notifications.

3. Responsible Content Moderation: The platform implements strict content moderation to prevent the spread of harmful or misleading information.

4. Transparent Algorithms: Users have visibility into how the content algorithm works, providing transparency about content recommendations.

The Role of Industry Standards and Regulations

Industry standards and regulations play a crucial role in promoting ethical practices in product design. Companies should align with established standards and comply with applicable regulations concerning data privacy, user consent, and digital well-being.

1. User Protection Laws: Comply with user protection laws and regulations, such as the General Data Protection Regulation (GDPR) and the Children's Online Privacy Protection Act (COPPA).

2. Self-Regulation: Industry bodies can establish self-regulatory frameworks that guide ethical practices in product design.

Conclusion

Ethical persuasion is essential in building habit-forming products that prioritize user well-being and create positive impacts on society. As product designers, we must remain mindful of the potential risks of unethical practices and strive to maintain the highest ethical standards in our work.

By embracing transparency, empowering users, prioritizing user well-being, and adhering to industry standards and regulations, product designers can create habit-forming products that enrich users' lives and foster meaningful, positive relationships with their audience.

As we navigate the complexities of product design and the psychology of persuasion, ethical considerations must remain at the forefront of our decision-making process. By putting the well-being of users first, we can build habit-forming products that go beyond short-term engagement metrics and contribute to a more responsible and sustainable digital ecosystem.

28. Unlocking User Motivation and Commitment

Habit hacking is the art of understanding and influencing user motivation and commitment to build habit-forming products. By tapping into the psychological drivers that shape human behavior, product designers can create experiences that resonate deeply with users and foster long-term engagement. In this chapter, we explore the principles of habit hacking, the psychology behind user motivation, and strategies for unlocking user commitment to build habit-forming products.

The Psychology of User Motivation

1. Intrinsic vs. Extrinsic Motivation: Intrinsic motivation stems from internal desires and interests, while extrinsic motivation is driven by external rewards or consequences. Habit-forming products aim to foster intrinsic motivation for sustained engagement.

2. The Self-Determination Theory: The self-determination theory suggests that individuals are motivated when they feel a sense of autonomy, competence, and relatedness. Habit-forming products should support users' autonomy and make them feel competent and connected.

3. The Goal-Setting Theory: Goal setting enhances motivation by providing a clear direction and sense of progress. Habit-forming products can leverage goal setting to drive user commitment.

The Principles of Habit Hacking

1. Triggers and Cues: Identify triggers and cues that prompt users to engage with the product. Triggers can be internal (emotions) or external (notifications), and cues act as reminders for desired behaviors.

2. Positive Reinforcement: Use positive reinforcement, such as rewards and achievements, to reinforce desired behaviors and motivate users to continue engaging with the product.

3. Feedback Loops: Provide timely and informative feedback to users, allowing them to track their progress and make adjustments to achieve their goals.

4. Gamification: Incorporate gamification elements, such as points, badges, and leaderboards, to create a sense of competition and motivate users to strive for mastery.

Strategies for Unlocking User Commitment

1. Personalization: Personalize the user experience based on individual preferences, goals, and behaviors. Customization enhances user commitment by making the product feel tailor-made for their needs.

2. Progress Tracking: Implement progress tracking features that allow users to monitor their achievements and witness their growth over time.

3. Social Support: Foster a sense of community where users can connect, share experiences, and support one another. Social support strengthens user commitment and accountability.

4. Habit Stacking: Encourage users to stack new habits onto existing routines, making it easier to adopt new behaviors.

Case Study: Fitness App and Habit Hacking

A fitness app can apply habit-hacking principles to unlock user commitment:

1. Personalized Workouts: The app offers personalized workout plans based on users' fitness levels and goals, keeping users engaged and motivated.

2. Goal Setting and Progress Tracking: Users can set fitness goals and track their progress, receiving positive reinforcement for achievements.

3. Social Support: The app includes a social community where users can share their fitness journeys, exchange tips, and encourage one another.

The Ethical Boundaries of Habit Hacking

While habit hacking can drive user commitment, it must be approached with ethical considerations to avoid manipulative practices and protect user well-being.

1. Informed Consent: Obtain explicit user consent for implementing habit hacking strategies, ensuring users understand how their behavior is influenced.

2. Autonomy and Empowerment: Empower users to control their engagement with the product and provide options to opt out of certain persuasive features.

3. Responsible Gamification: Use gamification responsibly, avoiding excessive competition or rewards that may lead to unhealthy behaviors.

Conclusion

Habit hacking is a powerful approach to unlocking user motivation and commitment, driving habit formation, and sustained engagement with products. By understanding the psychology of user motivation and applying habit-hacking principles, product designers can create experiences that deeply resonate with users and enrich their lives.

However, habit hacking must be approached ethically, prioritizing user autonomy, empowerment, and well-being. By aligning habit-hacking strategies with user interests and goals, product designers can build habit-forming products that foster positive behavioral change and create lasting impact in users' lives.

As the digital landscape evolves, habit hacking will continue to play a vital role in building products that genuinely connect with users, cultivate positive habits, and drive meaningful engagement. By maintaining ethical boundaries and putting users first, habit-forming products can become powerful tools for personal growth, empowerment, and positive transformation.

29. Data-Driven Habit Building

Data-driven habit building is the process of using metrics and analysis to understand user behavior and optimize product experiences for habit formation. By leveraging data insights, product designers can gain a deeper understanding of user habits, identify areas for improvement, and create more effective habit-forming products. In this chapter, we explore the significance of data-driven approaches, key metrics for habit analysis, and strategies for harnessing data to build habit-forming products.

The Power of Data in Habit Formation

Data plays a crucial role in habit formation by providing valuable insights into user behavior and product performance. With the right data-driven approach, product designers can create experiences that align with user needs and foster lasting engagement.

1. Behavior Analysis: Data allows product designers to analyze user behavior patterns, identify trigger points, and understand the factors that drive user engagement.

2. Personalization: Data-driven insights enable personalization, tailoring the product experience to individual preferences and habits.

3. Iterative Improvement: Continuous data analysis facilitates iterative product improvement, addressing user pain points and enhancing habit-forming elements.

4. Measuring Success: Data metrics provide a quantifiable measure of the product's success in fostering habit formation and user engagement.

Key Metrics for Habit Analysis

1. Retention Rate: The retention rate measures the percentage of users who continue to use the product over time. High retention rates indicate successful habit formation.

2. Habit Strength: Habit strength assesses the frequency and consistency of user engagement with the product. Strong habits result in regular and automatic usage.

3. Time Spent: Time spent metrics reveal the level of user engagement and the value users derive from the product.

4. Conversion Rate: The conversion rate measures the percentage of users who complete the desired action, such as signing up for an account or completing a purchase.

Strategies for Data-Driven Habit Building

1. Define Clear Objectives: Establish clear objectives for habit formation, outlining the specific behaviors and outcomes to measure.

2. Data Collection and Analysis: Implement data collection tools to track user interactions and behavior. Analyze data regularly to identify trends and patterns.

3. User Segmentation: Segment users based on behavior, preferences, and engagement levels to target personalized habit-building strategies.

4. A/B Testing: Conduct A/B tests to compare different product variations and identify which elements drive better habit formation.

Case Study: E-Commerce Platform and Data-Driven Habit Building

An e-commerce platform can use data-driven habit-building:

1. Personalized Product Recommendations: Leverage user data to provide personalized product recommendations, increasing user engagement and purchase frequency.

2. Retention Analysis: Analyze retention rates and identify factors that contribute to user churn. Addressing pain points can lead to higher retention and habitual usage.

Ethical Considerations in Data Collection

While data collection is valuable for habit building, it also raises ethical concerns related to user privacy and data security.

1. Anonymization: Anonymize user data to protect individual identities and ensure data security.

2. Data Transparency: Be transparent with users about data collection and usage practices, obtaining explicit consent when required.

3. Data Security: Implement robust data security measures to safeguard user information from unauthorized access.

Conclusion

Data-driven habit-building is a powerful tool for building habit-forming products that resonate with users and drive long-term engagement. By analyzing user behavior, measuring key metrics, and iteratively improving product experiences, product designers can create experiences that align with user needs and foster positive habits.

However, data-driven approaches must be carried out responsibly and ethically. Respect for user privacy, transparency in data practices, and a focus on user empowerment are essential principles in data-driven habit-building.

As technology continues to advance, data-driven habit-building will play an increasingly vital role in product design. By harnessing the power of data, product designers can create habit-forming products that enrich users' lives, drive positive behavioral change, and create lasting impact in the digital landscape.

30. The Habit-Forming Journey

The journey of building habit-forming products is filled with challenges, triumphs, and valuable lessons. In this chapter, we explore the success stories of companies that have created habit-forming products and the key lessons they learned along the way. By examining these case studies, product designers can gain insights into the strategies that drive habit formation and create products that resonate deeply with users.

Success Story: Instagram - The Power of Visual Storytelling

Instagram, a photo-sharing social platform, has become one of the most habit-forming products in the digital world. Its success can be attributed to several factors:

1. Simple and Intuitive User Interface: Instagram's clean and user-friendly interface makes it easy for users to navigate and share photos, promoting seamless engagement.

2. Visual Storytelling: The platform's focus on visual content allows users to tell stories through images, fostering emotional connections and frequent usage.

3. Social Interactions: Instagram's social features, such as likes, comments, and direct messaging, create a sense of community and social validation.

Lessons Learned

1. Emphasize User Experience: Prioritize user experience and design products that are intuitive, visually appealing, and easy to use.

2. Leverage Emotional Engagement: Foster emotional engagement by allowing users to express themselves creatively and form connections through content.

3. Cultivate Social Community: Build social features that encourage user interactions, fostering a sense of community and social validation.

Success Story: Slack - Reinventing Team Communication

Slack, a team communication and collaboration platform, revolutionized how teams communicate and work together. Its success can be attributed to:

1. Seamless Integration: Slack integrates with various productivity tools, streamlining team workflows and becoming an essential part of users' daily routines.

2. Real-Time Communication: The platform offers real-time messaging, making it easy for teams to communicate, collaborate, and stay in sync.

3. Personalization and Customization: Slack allows users to personalize their workspace with channels, notifications, and integrations, tailoring the platform to their needs.

Lessons Learned

1. Integrate with Existing Workflows: Design products that seamlessly integrate with users' existing workflows and add value to their daily routines.

2. Prioritize Real-Time Communication: Provide real-time communication features to facilitate quick and efficient interactions among users.

3. Empower Personalization: Allow users to customize their experience to suit their preferences and work style.

Success Story: Duolingo - Gamifying Language Learning

Duolingo, a language-learning app, gamified the language-learning experience, making it addictive and engaging. Its success can be attributed to:

1. Gamification: Duolingo incorporates gamification elements, such as points, streaks, and achievements, to motivate users and create a sense of progress.

2. Bite-Sized Lessons: The app offers bite-sized lessons that fit into users' busy schedules, encouraging consistent and regular practice.

3. Social Competition: Duolingo allows users to compete with friends, adding a social element that enhances motivation.

Lessons Learned

1. Gamify Learning: Gamification can enhance learning experiences by adding fun, motivation, and a sense of accomplishment.

2. Provide Microlearning: Break down learning content into smaller, manageable chunks to accommodate users' busy lifestyles.

3. Foster Social Learning: Incorporate social features that enable users to compete, collaborate, and support each other in their learning journey.

4. Success Story: Fitbit - Empowering Healthy Habits Fitbit, a fitness wearable company, has transformed how people approach health and fitness. Its success can be attributed to:

5. Goal Setting: Fitbit allows users to set fitness goals and tracks their progress, providing a sense of achievement and motivation.

6. Activity Tracking: The device tracks users' daily activities, encouraging them to stay active and maintain healthy habits.

7. Social Accountability: Fitbit's social features enable users to connect with friends, forming accountability circles that drive commitment.

Lessons Learned

1. Set Clear Goals: Enable users to set clear, achievable goals and provide tools to track their progress and celebrate milestones.

2. Use Data for Motivation: Leverage data to provide personalized feedback and insights that motivate users to stay committed to their health goals.

3. Foster Social Support: Create social features that allow users to share their progress, compete, and support each other in their health journey.

Conclusion

The habit-forming journey is a dynamic and evolving process, guided by user feedback, data insights, and a commitment to delivering value. Success stories of companies like Instagram, Slack, Duolingo, and Fitbit illustrate the power of understanding user behavior and designing experiences that align with user needs and desires.

By learning from these success stories and embracing the key lessons they offer, product designers can create habit-forming products that foster meaningful engagement and enrich users' lives. Prioritizing user experience, personalization, gamification, social interactions, and data-driven insights are foundational principles in building habit-forming products that stand the test of time.

As the landscape of digital products continues to evolve, the habit-forming journey remains an ongoing exploration of user behavior and motivation. By continuously iterating, learning, and adapting, product designers can create transformative experiences that go beyond mere usage—they can build products that become an integral part of users' lives and shape their behaviors in positive and empowering ways.

Epilogue

Congratulations! You have reached the end of "Hooked: How to Build Habit-Forming Products." Throughout this book, we have delved deep into the fascinating world of habit formation, exploring the psychology, neuroscience, and design principles that underpin the success of habit-forming products. We hope that this journey has enriched your understanding of the powerful impact of habit on human behavior and how to harness this knowledge to create products that captivate, engage, and empower users.

As you reflect on the insights, strategies, and success stories shared in this book, we encourage you to approach habit-forming product design with a sense of responsibility and ethics. The potential to shape user behavior is a privilege that must be handled with care. It is essential to prioritize user well-being, transparency, and consent when designing products that aim to build habits.

In this epilogue, we will recap some key takeaways from our exploration and provide you with a roadmap for applying these principles in your product design journey. Let us embark on a final journey together as we empower you to build habit-forming products that make a positive impact in the world.

Understanding the Power of Habit

At the core of habit-forming product design lies the understanding of how habits are formed and sustained. Habit formation is a gradual process that involves the interplay of triggers, actions, rewards, and investments. By aligning your product with the natural tendencies of the human brain, you can create experiences that effortlessly integrate into users' lives.

Navigating Ethical Boundaries

Building habit-forming products comes with great responsibility. As product designers, we must prioritize user well-being and avoid manipulative practices. Transparent communication, informed consent, and a focus on empowering users are fundamental principles in ethical product design.

Embracing User-Centric Design

The success of habit-forming products hinges on understanding and empathizing with users. By adopting a user-centric approach, you can identify their needs, pain points, and desires, crafting experiences that resonate deeply with their aspirations and goals.

Leveraging Data-Driven Insights

Data is a powerful ally in the quest to build habit-forming products. Analyzing user behavior and key metrics provides valuable insights into the effectiveness of your product and the habits it fosters. By leveraging data-driven insights, you can continuously improve your product to better serve your users.

Cultivating Positive Emotions

Emotions play a significant role in shaping user behavior. By designing experiences that evoke positive emotions and foster emotional connections, you can create products that users genuinely enjoy and look forward to using.

Balancing Gamification and Social Interactions

Gamification can enhance habit formation by adding elements of fun and motivation. However, it must be balanced with meaningful social interactions to create a sense of community and support. Encourage users to compete, collaborate, and learn from each other in their journey with your product.

Onboarding for Success

The onboarding experience is critical in forming lasting habits. By providing a smooth and guided onboarding process, you can set the stage for a positive user journey and long-term engagement.

Designing for Habitual Engagement

Habitual engagement goes beyond a one-time user experience. It involves cultivating a lasting relationship with users, fostering loyalty, and creating a product that seamlessly integrates into their daily routines.

Building Habit Ecosystems

Consider the broader context in which your product exists. By integrating your product into users' daily lives and complementary experiences, you can enhance its relevance and importance to users.

Reflecting on the Future

The future of habit-forming products is an ever-evolving landscape of innovation, challenges, and ethical considerations. Stay abreast of emerging technologies and trends, while remaining committed to creating products that contribute positively to society.

Empowered to Make a Difference

As we conclude our journey through "Hooked: How to Build Habit-Forming Products," we hope you feel empowered to make a difference in the world of product design. Habit-forming products have the potential to shape behaviors, support goals, and foster positive change. However, with this potential comes great responsibility.

Remember that behind every data point, every action, and every habit is a human being with unique needs, desires, and aspirations. Empathy and understanding are powerful tools that can guide you in creating products that truly resonate with users and enrich their lives.

Approach habit-forming product design with integrity, transparency, and a commitment to ethical practices. Let your passion for creating positive impact drive you to design products that inspire, empower, and bring joy to users.

As you continue your journey as a product designer, always remember that you have the power to shape the world through the products you create. Embrace this responsibility with humility, curiosity, and a continuous thirst for learning. Thank you for joining us in this exploration of habit-forming products. We are excited to see the positive impact you will make with your designs and the habits you will foster in the lives of millions.

Go forth and design with purpose, empathy, and the knowledge that your work has the potential to transform lives. May your future be filled with innovative ideas, meaningful connections, and a deep commitment to building habit-forming products that truly matter.

Wishing you all the best on your journey as you build a future of habit-forming products that leave a lasting mark on the world.

———

————

Milton Keynes UK
Ingram Content Group UK Ltd.
UKHW010650261023
431376UK00001B/120